HAL•LEONARD EASY JAZZ PLAY-ALONG

Book and CD for C, B♭, E♭ and Bass Clef Instruments

Volume 2

STANDARDS FOR STARTERS

HAL•LEONARD EASY JAZZ PLAY-ALONG
Book and CD for C, B♭, E♭ and Bass Clef Instruments

Volume 2

STANDARDS FOR STARTERS

18 Classics for Beginning Jazz Musicians

Recorded by Ric Probst at Tanner Monagle Studio
Piano: Mark Davis
Bass: Tom McGirr
Drums: Dave Bayles

ISBN 978-1-4584-1512-7

HAL•LEONARD® CORPORATION
7777 W. Bluemound Rd. P.O. Box 13819 Milwaukee, WI 53213

Visit Hal Leonard Online at
www.halleonard.com

CONTENTS

BOOK

CONTENTS

CD

DON'T GET AROUND MUCH ANYMORE

FROM SOPHISTICATED LADY

C VERSION

WORDS AND MUSIC BY DUKE ELLINGTON
AND BOB RUSSELL

* PLAY CUE NOTES FIRST AND LAST TIMES ONLY.

B♭7
Cmaj7
C7
F6
F♯m7
B7
Em7
E♭dim7
Dm7
Cmaj7
A7
D7
G7
1.–3.
C6
E♭7
Dm7
G7
4.
C6
G7
C6
G7
C6
A♭7
G7
C6

EXACTLY LIKE YOU

C VERSION

WORDS BY DOROTHY FIELDS
MUSIC BY JIMMY McHUGH

C7 F6 B♭7
C6 Am7 Dm7
Fm6 C6 E♭dim7 Dm7 G7
C6 D7
Dm7 G7
1., 2.
C6 Dm7 G7
3.
C6 E♭6 D♭maj7 Cmaj7

FLY ME TO THE MOON
(IN OTHER WORDS)

C VERSION

WORDS AND MUSIC BY
BART HOWARD

G7
Cmaj7
Fmaj7
Bm7♭5
E7
Am7
C♯dim7
Dm7
G7
E7
A7
TO CODA
1.
Dm7
C6
SOLO BREAK
2.
Dm7
G7
C6
Bm7♭5
E7
D.S. AL CODA
CODA
Dm7
C6
D♭maj7
Cmaj7

HAVE YOU MET MISS JONES?

FROM I'D RATHER BE RIGHT

C VERSION

WORDS BY LORENZ HART
MUSIC BY RICHARD RODGERS

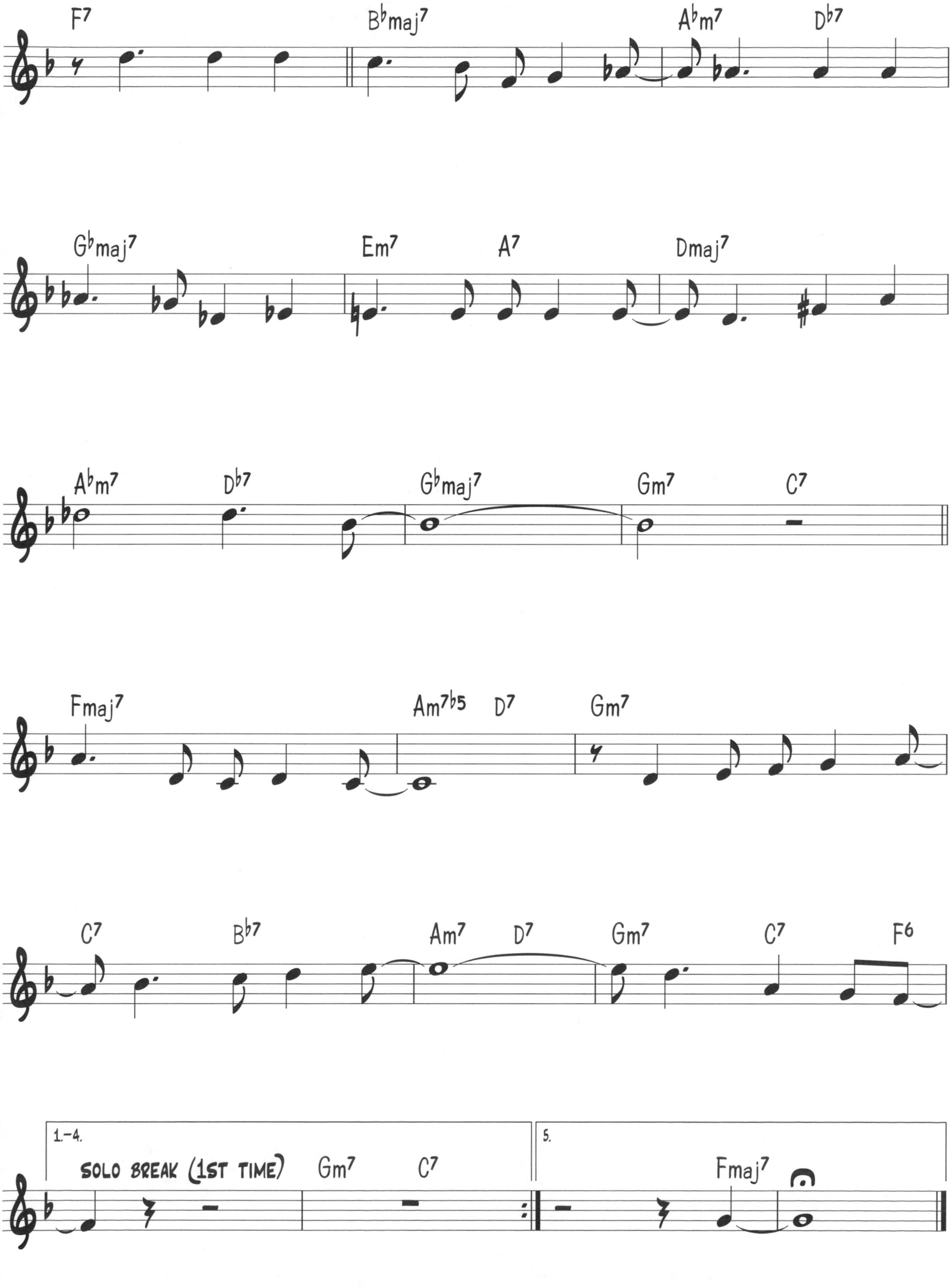
F7
B♭maj7
A♭m7
D♭7
G♭maj7
Em7
A7
Dmaj7
A♭m7
D♭7
G♭maj7
Gm7
C7
Fmaj7
Am7♭5
D7
Gm7
C7
B♭7
Am7
D7
Gm7
C7
F6
1.–4.
SOLO BREAK (1ST TIME)
Gm7
C7
5.
Fmaj7

HONEYSUCKLE ROSE

FROM AIN'T MISBEHAVIN'

C VERSION

WORDS BY ANDY RAZAF
MUSIC BY THOMAS "FATS" WALLER

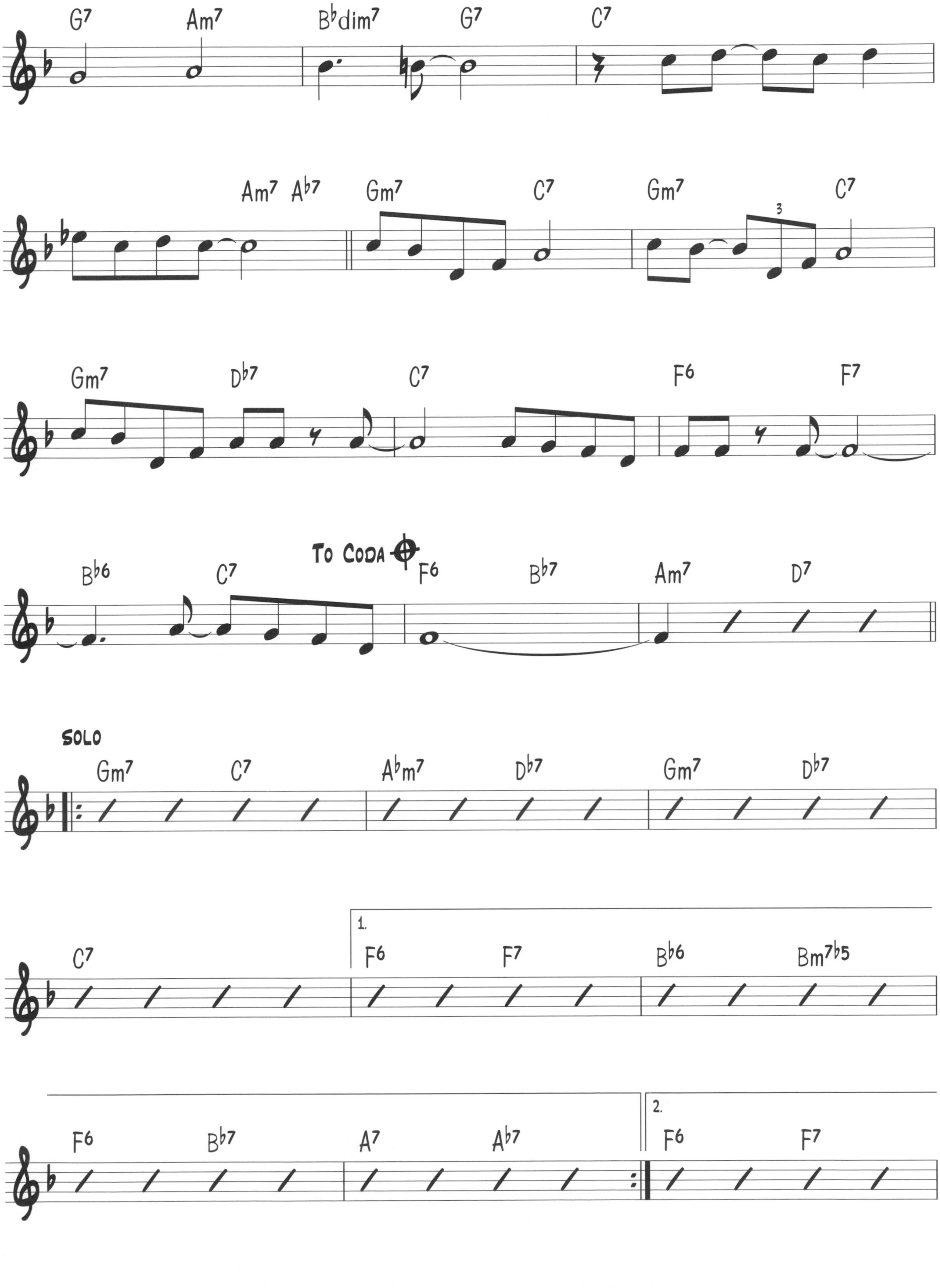
G7 Am7 B♭dim7 G7 C7
Am7 A♭7 Gm7 C7 Gm7 C7
Gm7 D♭7 C7 F6 F7
TO CODA
B♭6 C7 F6 B♭7 Am7 D7
SOLO
Gm7 C7 A♭m7 D♭7 Gm7 D♭7
C7
1.
F6 F7 B♭6 Bm7♭5
F6 B♭7 A7 A♭7
2.
F6 F7

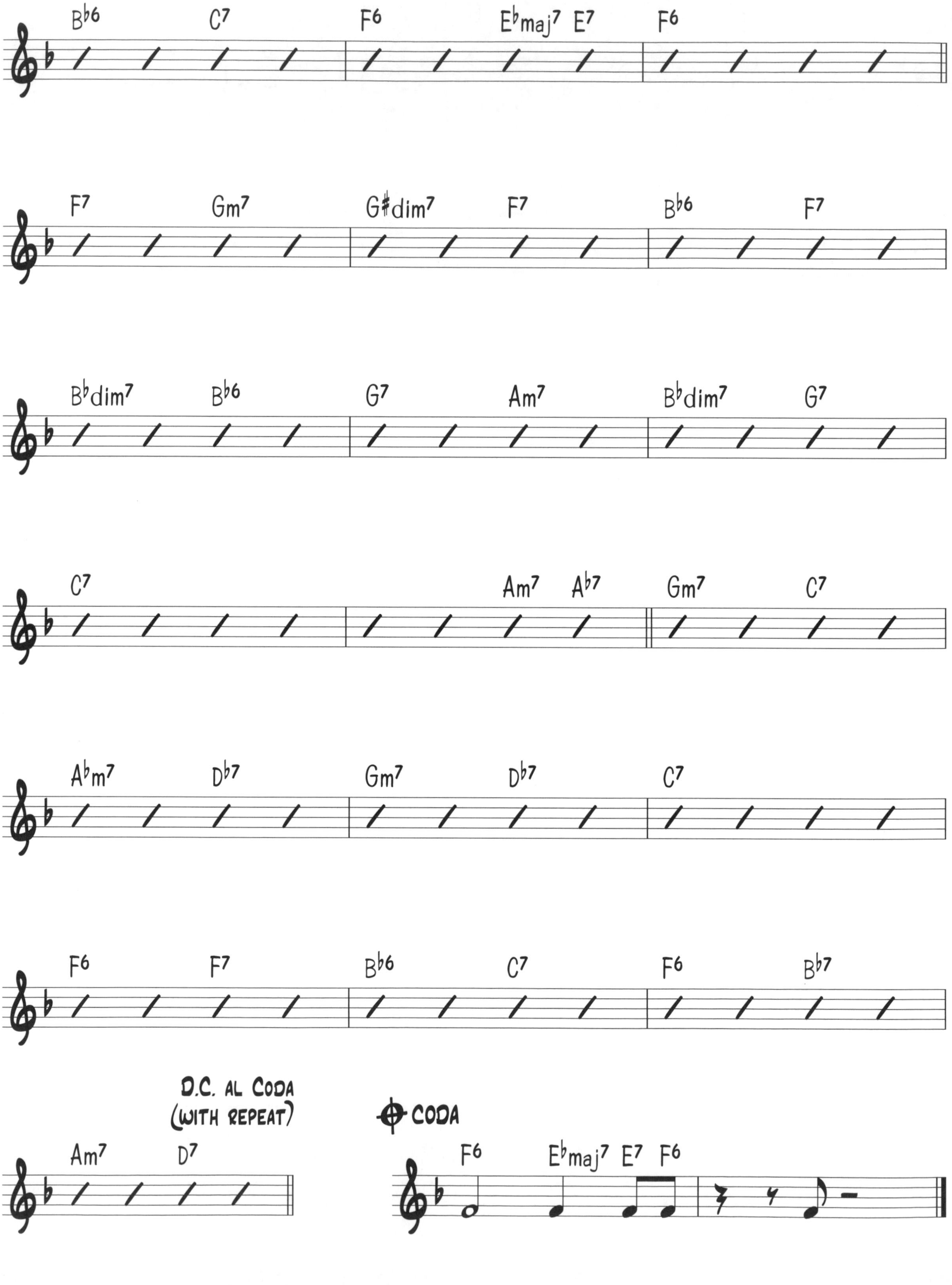
B♭6 C7 F6 E♭maj7 E7 F6
F7 Gm7 G♯dim7 F7 B♭6 F7
B♭dim7 B♭6 G7 Am7 B♭dim7 G7
C7 Am7 A♭7 Gm7 C7
A♭m7 D♭7 Gm7 D♭7 C7
F6 F7 B♭6 C7 F6 B♭7
D.C. al Coda
(with repeat)
Am7 D7
CODA
F6 E♭maj7 E7 F6

MY FAVORITE THINGS

FROM THE SOUND OF MUSIC

C VERSION

LYRICS BY OSCAR HAMMERSTEIN II
MUSIC BY RICHARD RODGERS

INTRODUCTION
MEDIUM JAZZ WALTZ

Em
Cmaj7
Am7
D7
Gmaj7
C6
Gmaj7
Cmaj7
F#m7b5
B7
Emaj7
Amaj7
Am7
D7
Gmaj7
Cmaj7
Gmaj7
Cmaj7
F#m7b5
B7

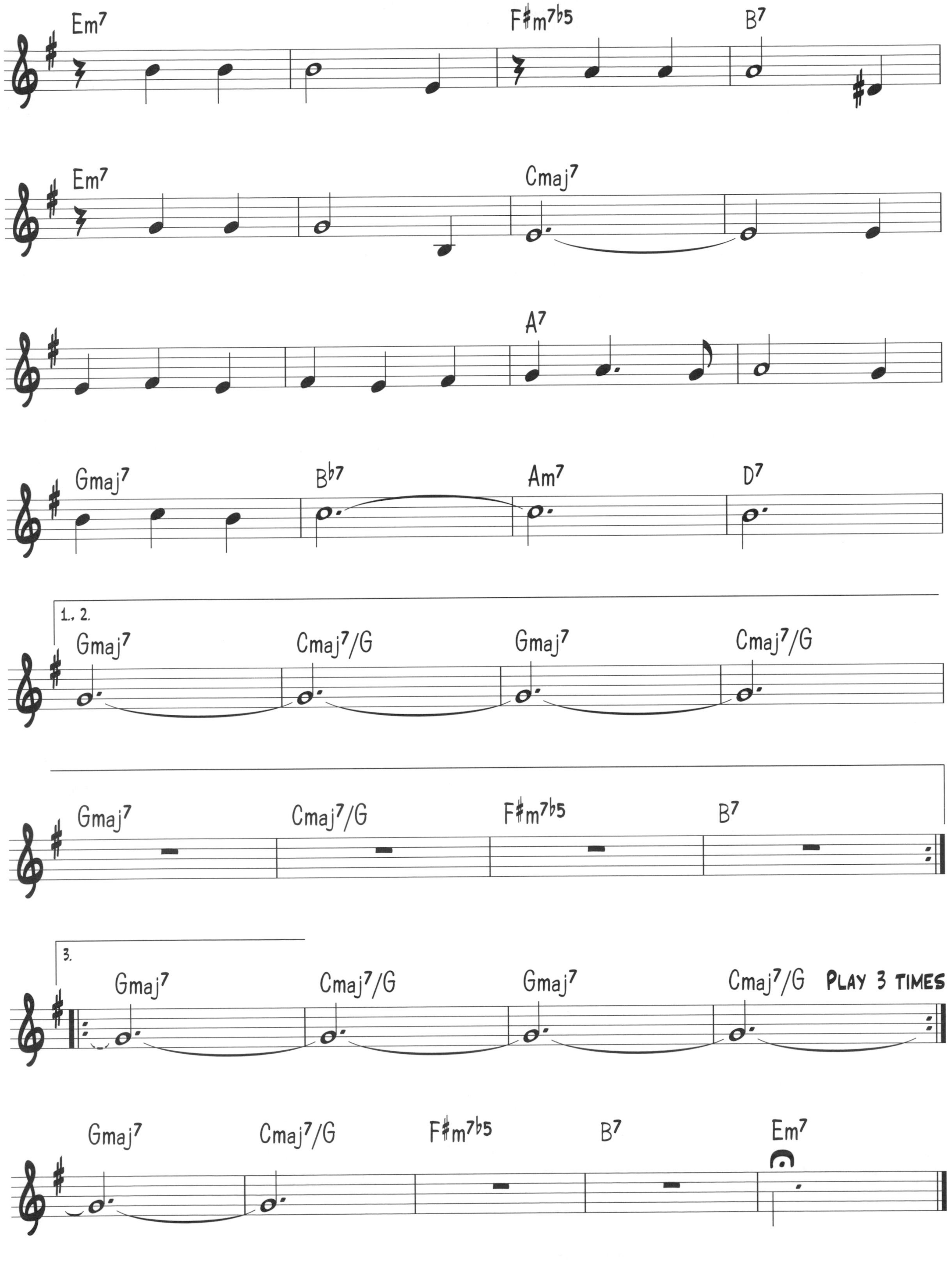
Em7
F#m7b5
B7
Em7
Cmaj7
A7
Gmaj7
Bb7
Am7
D7
1., 2.
Gmaj7
Cmaj7/G
Gmaj7
Cmaj7/G
Gmaj7
Cmaj7/G
F#m7b5
B7
3.
Gmaj7
Cmaj7/G
Gmaj7
Cmaj7/G
PLAY 3 TIMES
Gmaj7
Cmaj7/G
F#m7b5
B7
Em7

I REMEMBER YOU

FROM THE PARAMOUNT PICTURE THE FLEET'S IN

C VERSION

WORDS BY JOHNNY MERCER
MUSIC BY VICTOR SCHERTZINGER

Em7 A7 Dmaj7 Dm7 G7
Cmaj7 Abdim7 Gm6 C7 Fmaj7 Bm7 E7
Fmaj7 Bb7 Am7 D7 Gm7
Eb7 F6 Bm7b5 Bb7
1., 2.
Am7 Ab7 Gm7 C7 F6
SOLO BREAK (1ST TIME)
3.
Am7 Ab7 Gm7 C7 Abmaj7 F7 Bbm7 Eb7
Am7 Ab7 Gm7 C7 F6 G/F

IF I SHOULD LOSE YOU

FROM THE PARAMOUNT PICTURE ROSE OF THE RANCHO

C VERSION

WORDS AND MUSIC BY LEO ROBIN
AND RALPH RAINGER

INTRODUCTION
MEDIUM LATIN

D7 A♭7 F♯dim7/G Gm7 Am7 D7
F♯dim7/G Gm7 Fm7 B♭7 D/E♭ E♭maj7
Fm7 B♭7 B♭7/E♭ E♭maj7 B♭/D
Cm7 F7 B♭dim7 B♭maj7
D7 Gm7 Cm7 F7
1., 2.
B♭6 Am7♭5 D7
3.
Bmaj7
B♭maj7

IT COULD HAPPEN TO YOU

FROM THE PARAMOUNT PICTURE AND THE ANGELS SING

C VERSION

WORDS BY JOHNNY BURKE
MUSIC BY JAMES VAN HEUSEN

Gm7 Bm7b5 E7 Fmaj7
Bb7 A7 D7 Gm7
Eb7 Fmaj7 Bb7 Am7b5 D7
Gm7 C7
1., 2.
F6 D9 Gm7
C7
3.
F6 D7 Gm C7 Am7
Ab7 Gm7 C7 Am7 D7 Gm7
C7 Gbmaj7 Fmaj7

MOON RIVER

FROM THE PARAMOUNT PICTURE BREAKFAST AT TIFFANY'S

C VERSION

WORDS BY JOHNNY MERCER
MUSIC BY HERNY MANCINI

Fmaj7 Cmaj7 Bm7b5 E7
Am7 F#m7b5 F7
Cmaj7 Fmaj7 Cmaj7 Fmaj7
Cmaj7 Am7 Ab7 G7
TO CODA
1.
SOLO BREAK
Cmaj7 Bbmaj7 Cmaj7 Bbmaj7 Cmaj7 Bbmaj7
G7
2.
Cmaj7 G7
3.
D.S. AL CODA
Cmaj7 G7
CODA
Cmaj7 Bbmaj7 Cmaj7 Bbmaj7
Cmaj7 Bbmaj7 Cmaj7 Bbmaj7 Abmaj7 G7 Cmaj7

ON A SLOW BOAT TO CHINA

C VERSION

BY FRANK LOESSER

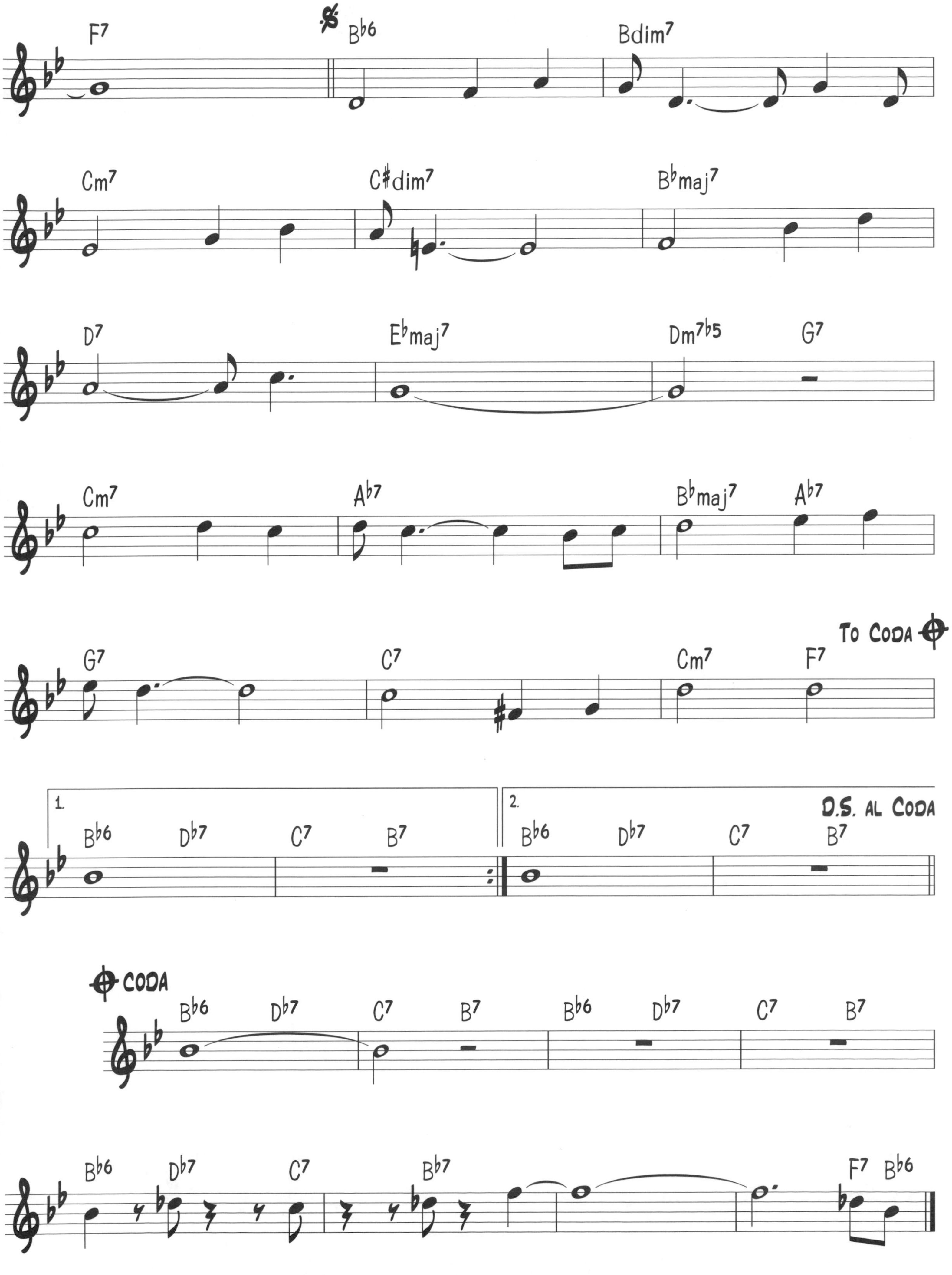
F7 B♭6 Bdim7
Cm7 C♯dim7 B♭maj7
D7 E♭maj7 Dm7♭5 G7
Cm7 A♭7 B♭maj7 A♭7
To Coda
G7 C7 Cm7 F7
1.
B♭6 D♭7 C7 B7
2.
D.S. al Coda
B♭6 D♭7 C7 B7
CODA
B♭6 D♭7 C7 B7 B♭6 D♭7 C7 B7
B♭6 D♭7 C7 B♭7 F7 B♭6

OUT OF NOWHERE

FROM THE PARAMOUNT PICTURE DUDE RANCH

C VERSION

WORDS BY EDWARD HEYMAN
MUSIC BY JOHNNY GREEN

C7
Bm7
E7
Am7
Bm7
E7
Am7
F7
To Coda
Bm7
Bdim
Am7
D7
1.–3.
G6
G#dim
Am7
D7
4.
G6
G#dim
Am7
D7
D.C. al Coda
Coda
Bm7
B♭dim
Am7
D7
Bm7
B♭dim
Am7
D7
Bm7
B♭dim
Am7
D7
G6
F7
G♭7
G7

SOFTLY AS IN A MORNING SUNRISE

FROM THE NEW MOON

C VERSION

LYRICS BY OSCAR HAMMERSTEIN II
MUSIC BY SIGMUND ROMBERG

E♭maj7
Gm7♭5
C7
Fm7
D7
Dm7♭5
A♭7
Cm6
Dm7♭5
G7
Cm6
A♭7
G7
Cm6
1., 2.
Dm7♭5
G7
Cm6
Dm7♭5/C
3.
Dm7♭5
G7
Cm6

SPEAK LOW

FROM THE MUSICAL PRODUCTION ONE TOUCH OF VENUS

C VERSION

WORDS BY OGDEN NASH
MUSIC BY KURT WEILL

Gm7 C7 Gm7
C7 Am7 D7
B♭m7 E♭7 B♭m7
E♭7 Am7 D7 Gm7 C7
F6 Fm7
D♭7 E♭maj7
D♭7 C7

Gm7 C7 Gm7
3
C7 Gm7 C7
3
3
Am7 D7 B♭m7 E♭7
3
Fmaj7 E♭7 D7 G7
C7 F6 B♭7 Am7 D7
1.
2.
Am7 D7 G7
C7 F6 Fmaj7

THE WAY YOU LOOK TONIGHT

FROM SWING TIME

C VERSION

WORDS BY DOROTHY FIELDS
MUSIC BY JEROME KERN

* SKIP CUE NOTES ON THE SOLOS.

Fm7
B♭7
E♭maj7
D♭7
C7
Fm7
B♭7
B♭m7
E♭7
A♭maj7
Fm7
B♭7
E♭6
Cm7
Fm7
B♭7
E♭maj7
Cm7
A♭m7
D♭7
G♭maj7
Gdim7
A♭m7
D♭7
G♭maj7
B♭m7
Adim7
A♭m7
D♭7
G♭maj7
Gdim7
A♭m7
D♭7

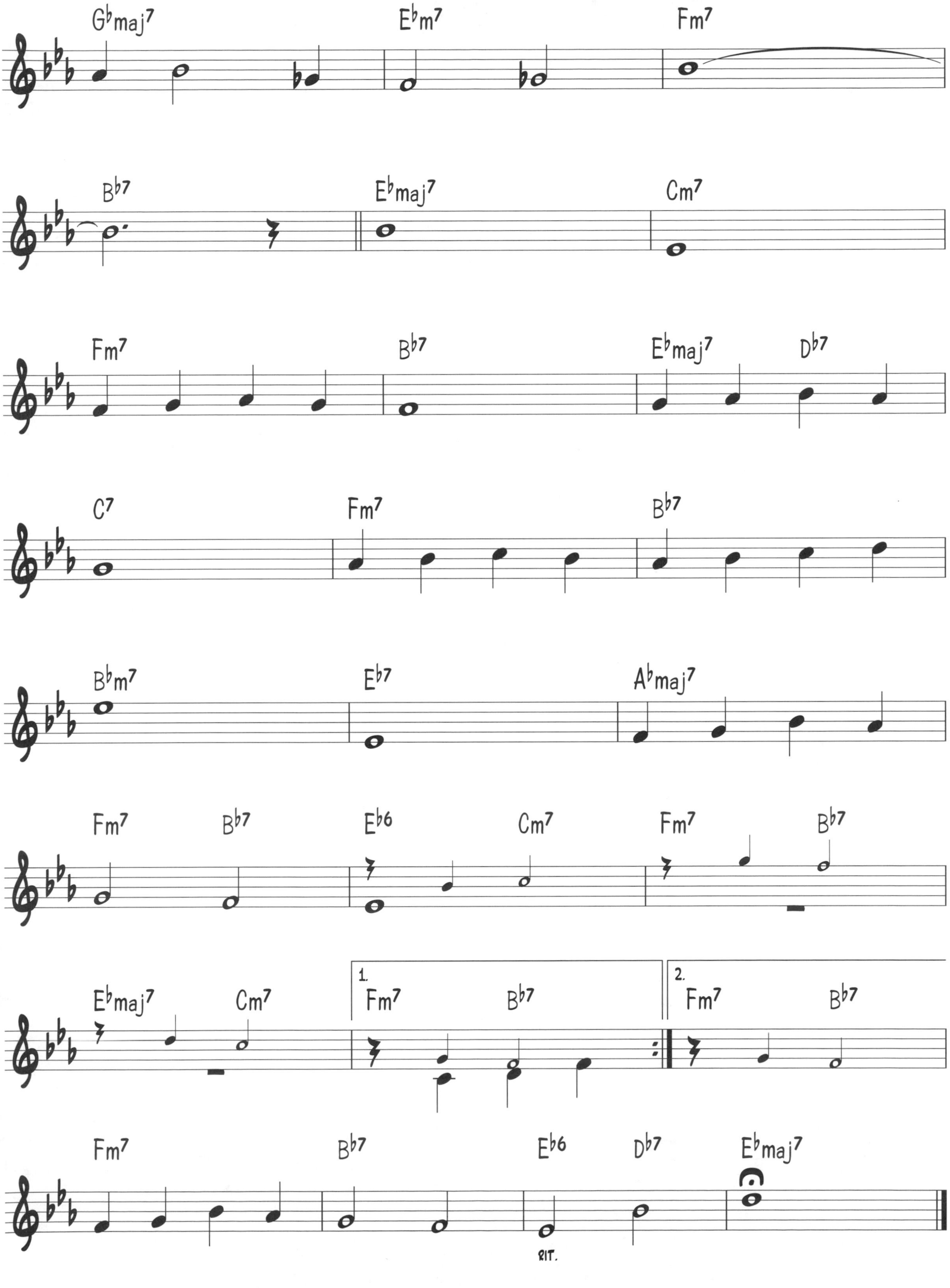
G♭maj7
E♭m7
Fm7
B♭7
E♭maj7
Cm7
Fm7
B♭7
E♭maj7
D♭7
C7
Fm7
B♭7
B♭m7
E♭7
A♭maj7
Fm7
B♭7
E♭6
Cm7
Fm7
B♭7
E♭maj7
Cm7
1.
Fm7
B♭7
2.
Fm7
B♭7
Fm7
B♭7
E♭6
D♭7
E♭maj7
RIT.

THE VERY THOUGHT OF YOU

C VERSION

WORDS AND MUSIC BY
RAY NOBLE

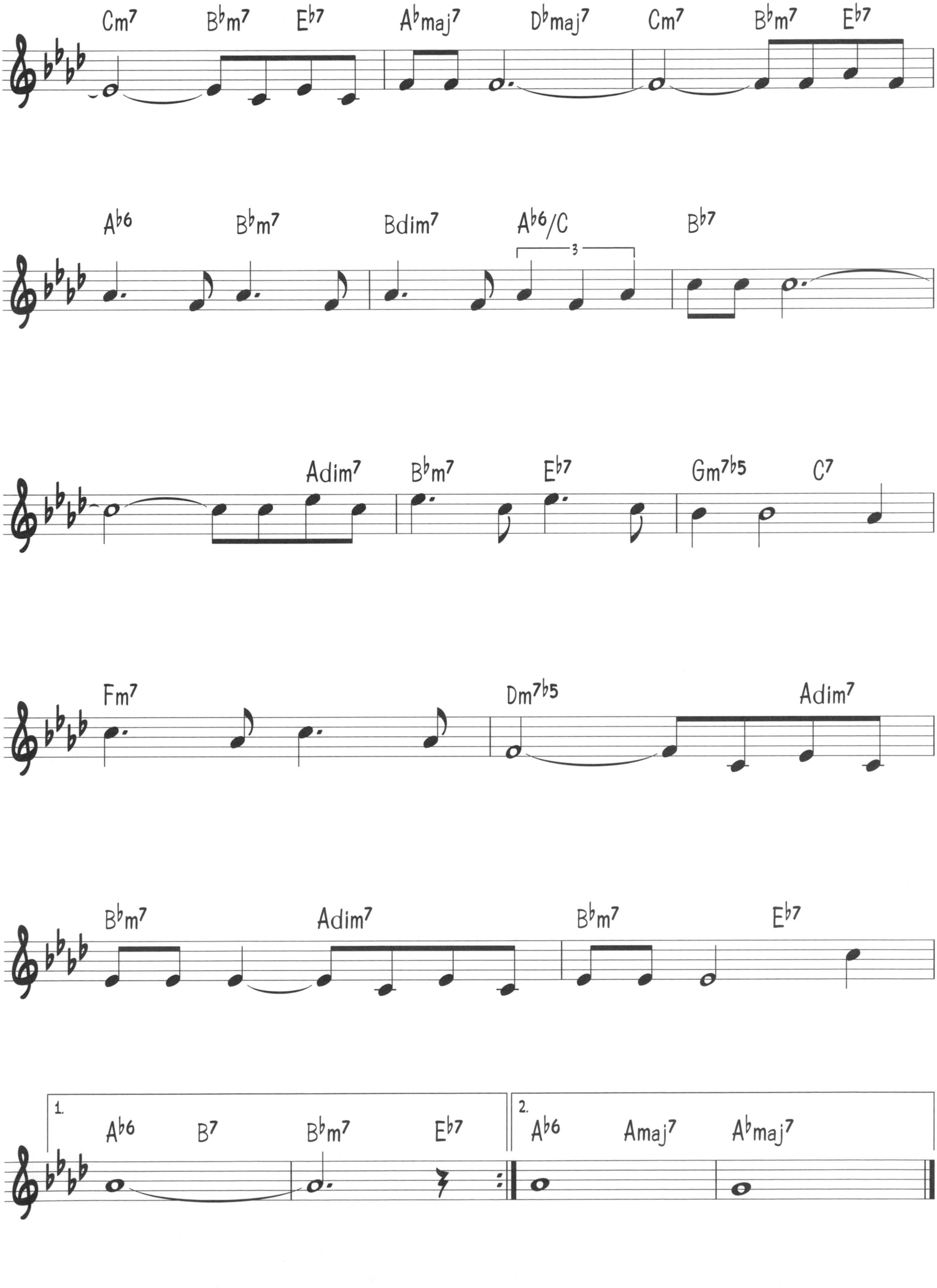
Cm7 B♭m7 E♭7 A♭maj7 D♭maj7 Cm7 B♭m7 E♭7
A♭6 B♭m7 Bdim7 A♭6/C B♭7
3
Adim7 B♭m7 E♭7 Gm7♭5 C7
Fm7 Dm7♭5 Adim7
B♭m7 Adim7 B♭m7 E♭7
1.
A♭6 B7 B♭m7 E♭7
2.
A♭6 Amaj7 A♭maj7

WATCH WHAT HAPPENS

FROM THE UMBRELLAS OF CHERBOURG

C VERSION

MUSIC BY MICHEL LEGRAND
ORIGINAL FRENCH TEXT BY JACQUES DEMY
ENGLISH LYRICS BY NORMAN GIMBEL

C7
Fmaj7
3
3
Fm7
B♭7
E♭maj7
3
F7
3
3
Fm7
B♭7
3
E♭6
E6
D6
E♭6
E6
D6
1., 2.
E♭6
Fm7
B♭7
3.
E♭6
E6
E/D
E♭maj7

YESTERDAYS

FROM ROBERTA

C VERSION

WORDS BY OTTO HARBACH
MUSIC BY JEROME KERN

INTRODUCTION
SLOW LATIN

B♭ Instruments

DON'T GET AROUND MUCH ANYMORE

FROM SOPHISTICATED LADY

B♭ VERSION

WORDS AND MUSIC BY DUKE ELLINGTON
AND BOB RUSSELL

* PLAY CUE NOTES FIRST AND LAST TIMES ONLY.

C7 Dmaj7 D7
G6 G#m7 C#7 F#m7 Fdim7
Em7 Dmaj7
B7 E7
A7 1.–3. D6 F7 Em7 A7
4. D6 A7 D6
A7 D6 Bb7 A7 D6

EXACTLY LIKE YOU

B♭ VERSION

WORDS BY DOROTHY FIELDS
MUSIC BY JIMMY McHUGH

D7
G6
C7
D6
Bm7
Em7
Gm6
D6
Fdim7
Em7
A7
D6
E7
Em7
A7
1., 2.
D6
Em7
A7
3.
D6
F6
E♭maj7
Dmaj7

FLY ME TO THE MOON
(IN OTHER WORDS)

Bb VERSION

WORDS AND MUSIC BY
BART HOWARD

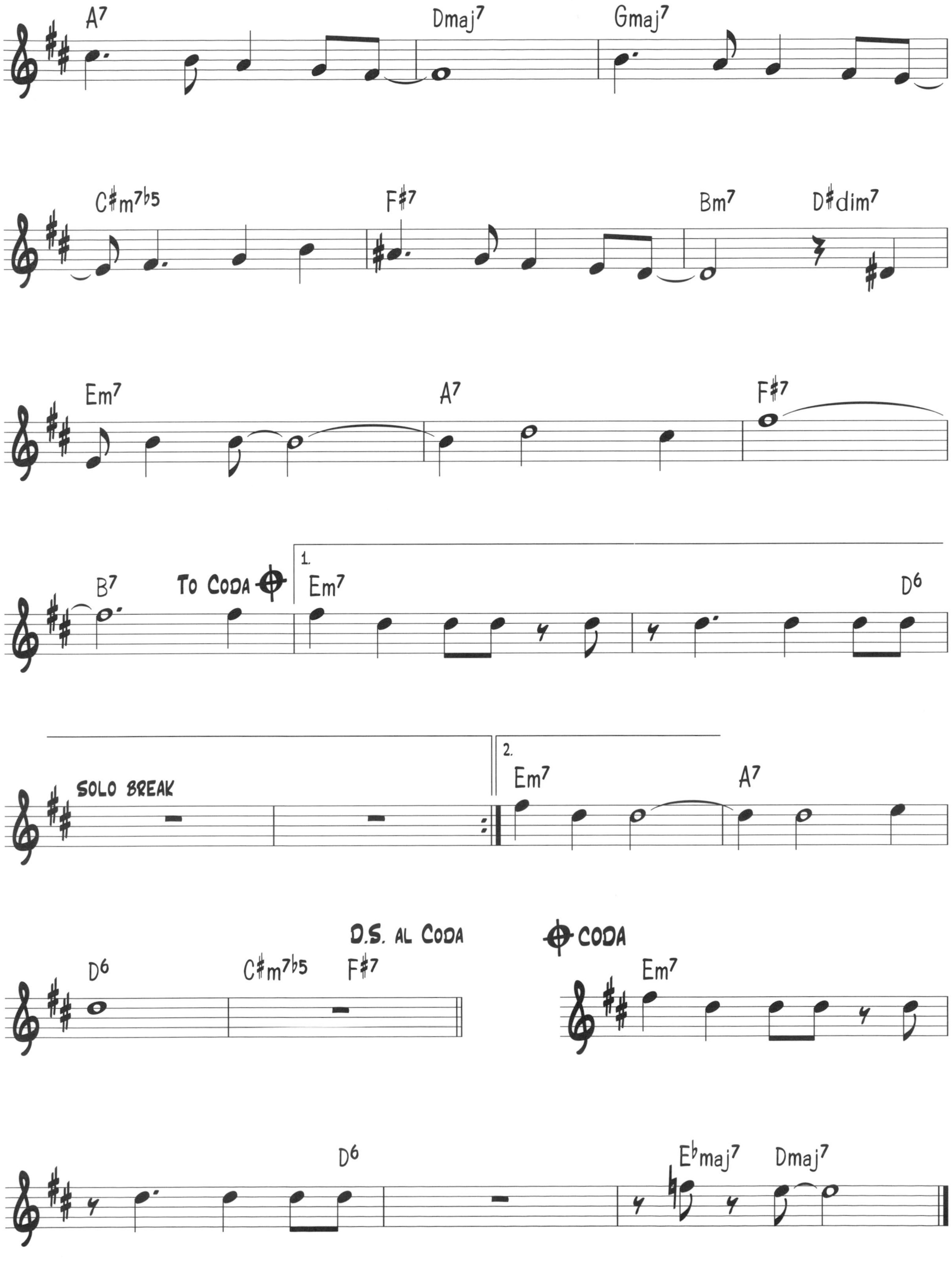
A7
Dmaj7
Gmaj7
C#m7b5
F#7
Bm7
D#dim7
Em7
A7
F#7
B7
TO CODA
1.
Em7
D6
SOLO BREAK
2.
Em7
A7
D.S. AL CODA
CODA
D6
C#m7b5
F#7
Em7
D6
Ebmaj7
Dmaj7

HAVE YOU MET MISS JONES?

FROM I'D RATHER BE RIGHT

B♭ VERSION

WORDS BY LORENZ HART
MUSIC BY RICHARD RODGERS

MEDIUM SWING

G7
Cmaj7
B♭m7
E♭7
A♭maj7
F♯m7
B7
Emaj7
B♭m7
E♭7
A♭maj7
Am7
D7
Gmaj7
Bm7♭5
E7
Am7
D7
C7
Bm7
E7
Am7
D7
G6
1.–4.
SOLO BREAK (1ST TIME)
Am7
D7
5.
Gmaj7

HONEYSUCKLE ROSE

FROM AIN'T MISBEHAVIN'

B♭ VERSION

WORDS BY ANDY RAZAF
MUSIC BY THOMAS "FATS" WALLER

A7 Bm7 Cdim7 A7 D7
Bm7 Bb7 Am7 D7 Am7 D7
3
Am7 Eb7 D7 G6 G7
To Coda
C6 D7 G6 C7 Bm7 E7
SOLO
Am7 D7 Bbm7 Eb7 Am7 Eb7
D7
1.
G6 G7 C6 C#m7b5
G6 C7 B7 Bb7
2.
G6 G7

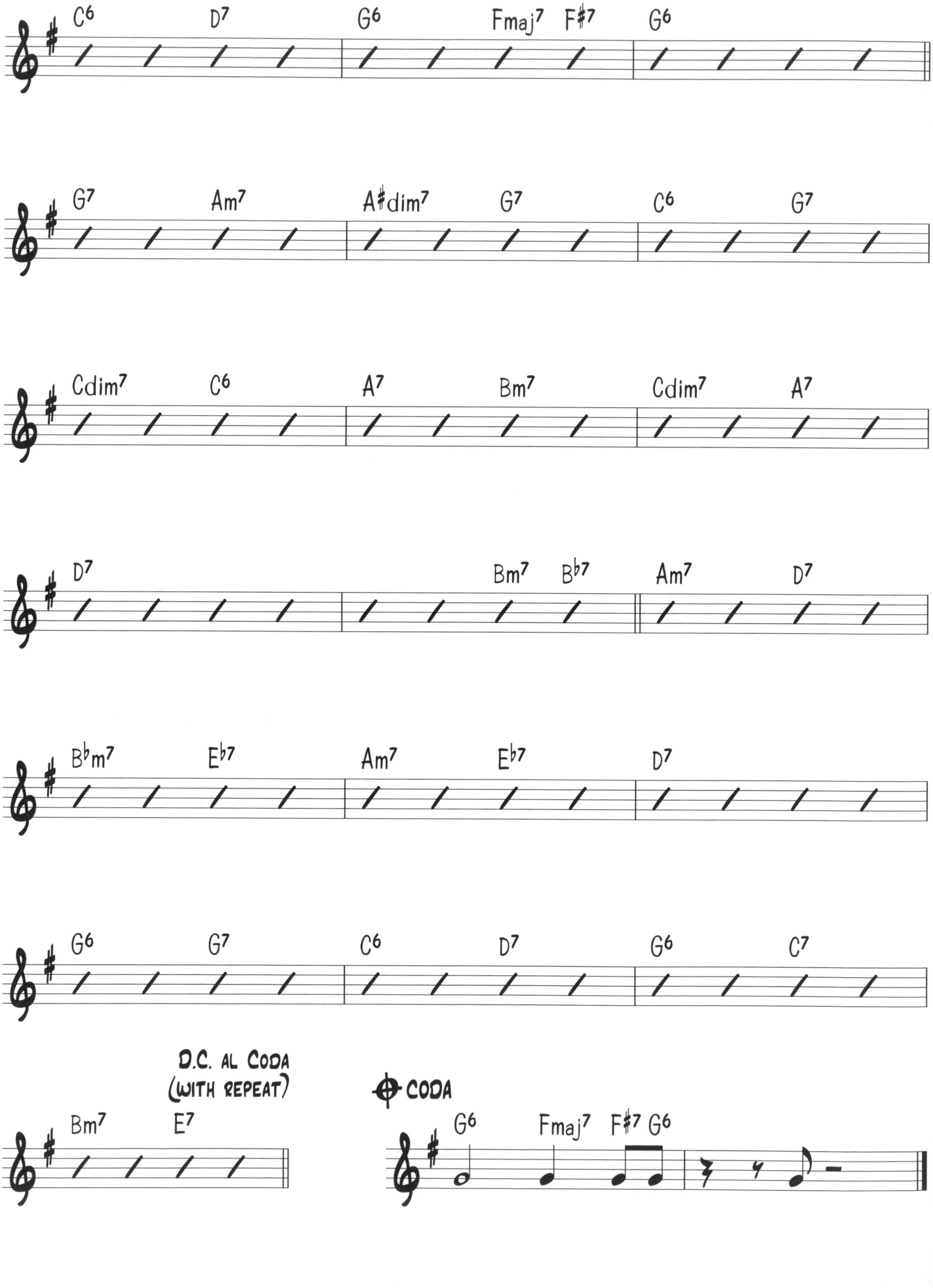
C6 D7 G6 Fmaj7 F#7 G6
G7 Am7 A#dim7 G7 C6 G7
Cdim7 C6 A7 Bm7 Cdim7 A7
D7 Bm7 Bb7 Am7 D7
Bbm7 Eb7 Am7 Eb7 D7
G6 G7 C6 D7 G6 C7
D.C. AL CODA
(WITH REPEAT)
Bm7 E7
CODA
G6 Fmaj7 F#7 G6

MY FAVORITE THINGS

FROM THE SOUND OF MUSIC

Bb VERSION

LYRICS BY OSCAR HAMMERSTEIN II
MUSIC BY RICHARD RODGERS

F♯m
Dmaj7
Bm7
E7
Amaj7
D6
Amaj7
Dmaj7
G♯m7♭5
C♯7
F♯maj7
Bmaj7
Bm7
E7
Amaj7
Dmaj7
Amaj7
Dmaj7
G♯m7♭5
C♯7

F#m7
G#m7b5
C#7
F#m7
Dmaj7
B7
Amaj7
C7
Bm7
E7
1., 2.
Amaj7
Dmaj7/A
Amaj7
Dmaj7/A
Amaj7
Dmaj7/A
G#m7b5
C#7
3.
Amaj7
Dmaj7/A
Amaj7
Dmaj7/A
PLAY 3 TIMES
Amaj7
Dmaj7/A
G#m7b5
C#7
F#m7

I REMEMBER YOU

FROM THE PARAMOUNT PICTURE THE FLEET'S IN

B♭ VERSION

WORDS BY JOHNNY MERCER
MUSIC BY VICTOR SCHERTZINGER

F#m7 B7 Emaj7 Em7 A7
Dmaj7 Bbdim7 Am6 D7 Gmaj7 C#m7 F#7
Gmaj7 C7 Bm7 E7 Am7
F7 G6 C#m7b5 C7
1., 2.
Bm7 Bb7 Am7 D7 G6
SOLO BREAK (1ST TIME)
3.
Bm7 Bb7 Am7 D7 Bbmaj7 G7 Cm7 F7
Bm7 Bb7 Am7 D7 G6 A/G

IF I SHOULD LOSE YOU

FROM THE PARAMOUNT PICTURE ROSE OF THE RANCHO

B♭ VERSION

WORDS AND MUSIC BY LEO ROBIN
AND RALPH RAINGER

E7 Bb7 G#dim7/A Am7 Bm7 E7
G#dim7/A Am7 Gm7 C7 E/F Fmaj7
Gm7 C7 C7/F Fmaj7 C/E
Dm7 G7 Cdim7 Cmaj7
E7 Am7 Dm7 G7
1., 2.
C6 Bm7b5 E7
3.
C#maj7
Cmaj7

IT COULD HAPPEN TO YOU

FROM THE PARAMOUNT PICTURE AND THE ANGELS SING

B♭ VERSION

WORDS BY JOHNNY BURKE
MUSIC BY JAMES VAN HEUSEN

Am7 C#m7b5 F#7 Gmaj7
C7 B7 E7 Am7
F7 Gmaj7 C7 Bm7b5 E7
Am7 D7
1., 2.
G6 E9 Am7
D7
3.
G6 E7 Am D7 Bm7
Bb7 Am7 D7 Bm7 E7 Am7
D7 Abmaj7 Gmaj7

MOON RIVER

FROM THE PARAMOUNT PICTURE BREAKFAST AT TIFFANY'S

Bb VERSION

WORDS BY JOHNNY MERCER
MUSIC BY HERNY MANCINI

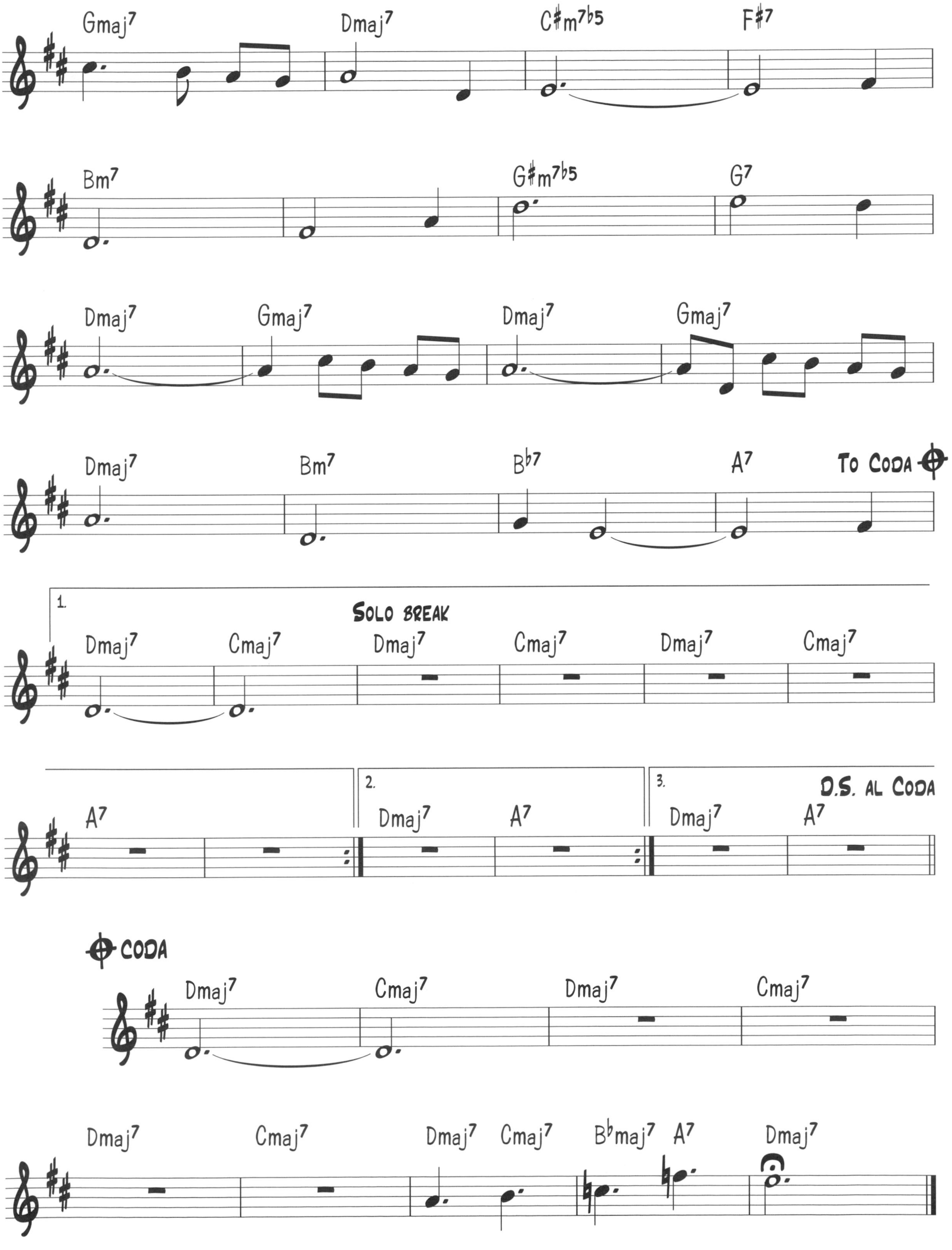
Gmaj7 Dmaj7 C#m7b5 F#7
Bm7 G#m7b5 G7
Dmaj7 Gmaj7 Dmaj7 Gmaj7
Dmaj7 Bm7 Bb7 A7
To Coda
1.
Solo break
Dmaj7 Cmaj7 Dmaj7 Cmaj7 Dmaj7 Cmaj7
A7
2.
Dmaj7 A7
3.
D.S. al Coda
Dmaj7 A7
Coda
Dmaj7 Cmaj7 Dmaj7 Cmaj7
Dmaj7 Cmaj7 Dmaj7 Cmaj7 Bbmaj7 A7 Dmaj7

ON A SLOW BOAT TO CHINA

B♭ VERSION

BY FRANK LOESSER

INTRODUCTION
MEDIUM SHUFFLE

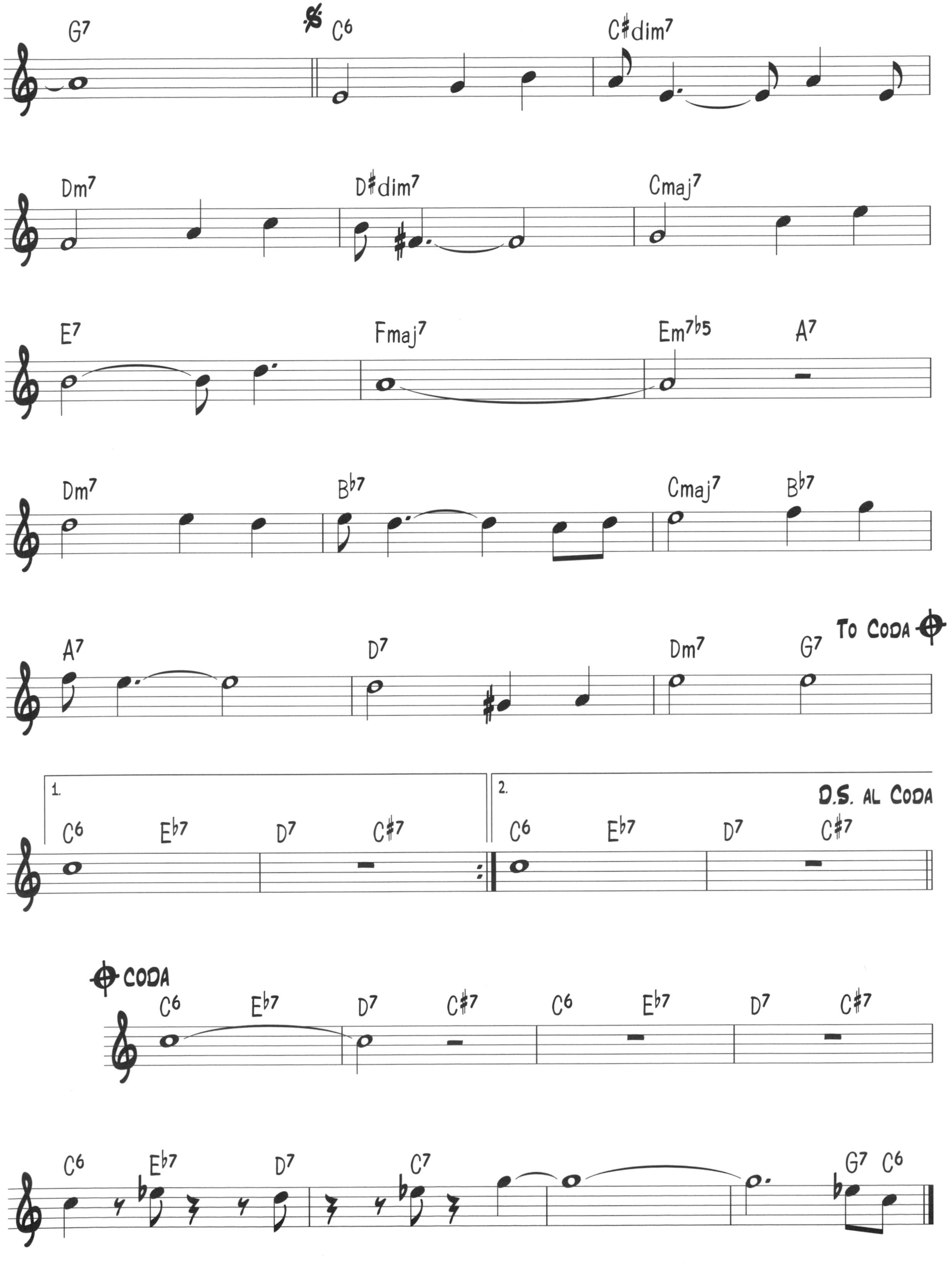
G7
C6
C#dim7
Dm7
D#dim7
Cmaj7
E7
Fmaj7
Em7b5
A7
Dm7
Bb7
Cmaj7
Bb7
A7
D7
Dm7
G7
To Coda
1.
C6
Eb7
D7
C#7
2.
D.S. al Coda
C6
Eb7
D7
C#7
Coda
C6
Eb7
D7
C#7
C6
Eb7
D7
C#7
C6
Eb7
D7
C7
G7
C6

OUT OF NOWHERE

FROM THE PARAMOUNT PICTURE DUDE RANCH

B♭ VERSION

WORDS BY EDWARD HEYMAN
MUSIC BY JOHNNY GREEN

D7
C#m7
F#7
Bm7
C#m7
F#7
Bm7
TO CODA
G7
C#m7
C#dim
Bm7
E7
1.-3.
A6
A#dim
Bm7
E7
4.
D.C. AL CODA
A6
A#dim
Bm7
E7
CODA
C#m7
Cdim
Bm7
E7
C#m7
Cdim
Bm7
E7
C#m7
Cdim
Bm7
E7
A6
G7
Ab7
A7

SOFTLY AS IN A MORNING SUNRISE

FROM THE NEW MOON

B♭ VERSION

LYRICS BY OSCAR HAMMERSTEIN II
MUSIC BY SIGMUND ROMBERG

INTRODUCTION
LIGHT LATIN-ROCK

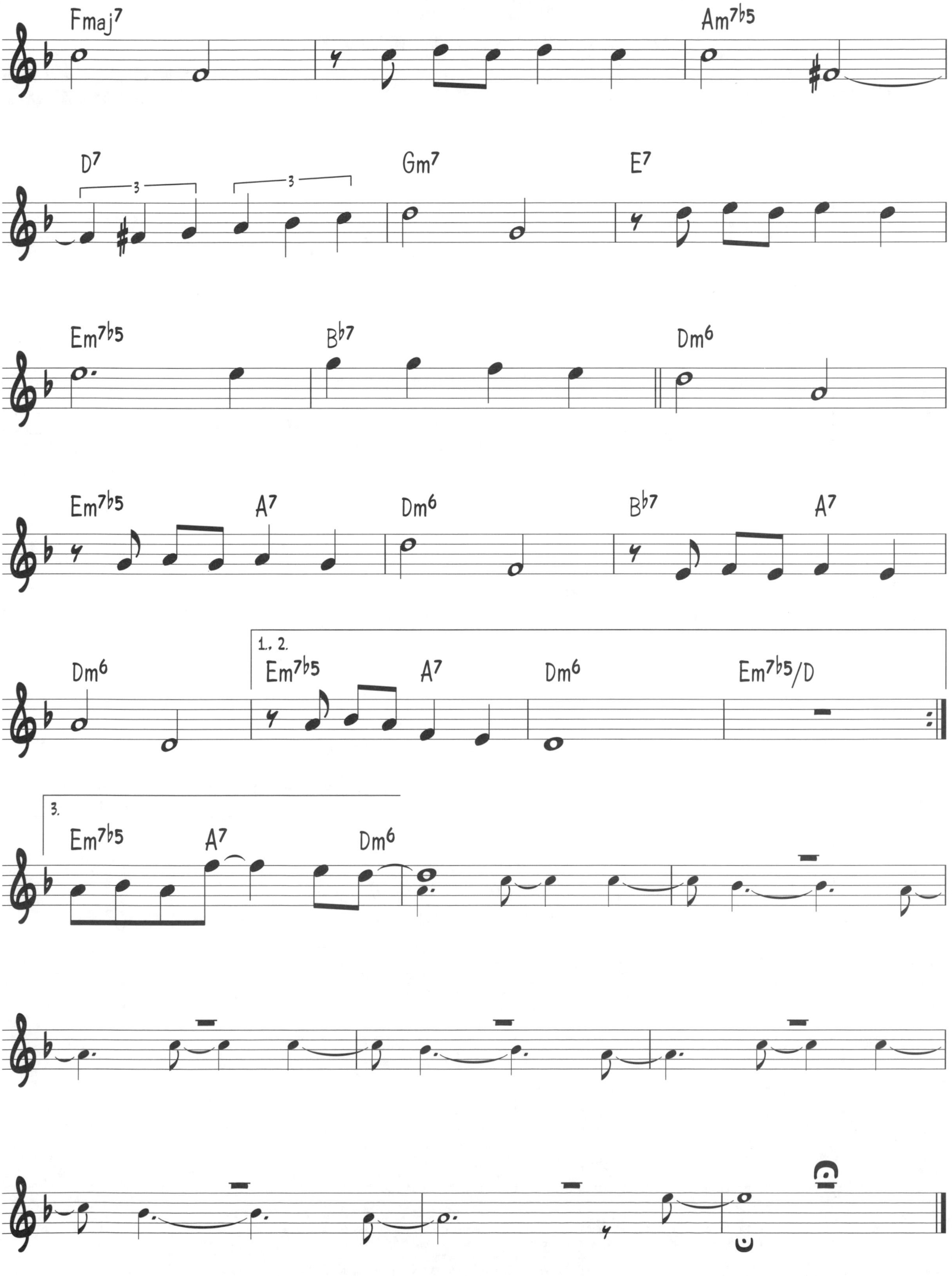
Fmaj7
Am7♭5
D7
3
3
Gm7
E7
Em7♭5
B♭7
Dm6
Em7♭5
A7
Dm6
B♭7
A7
Dm6
1., 2.
Em7♭5
A7
Dm6
Em7♭5/D
3.
Em7♭5
A7
Dm6

SPEAK LOW

FROM THE MUSICAL PRODUCTION ONE TOUCH OF VENUS

B♭ VERSION

WORDS BY OGDEN NASH
MUSIC BY KURT WEILL

Am7
D7
3
Am7
3
D7
Bm7
E7
Cm7
F7
3
Cm7
F7
3
Bm7
E7
3
Am7
D7
3
G6
Gm7
3
E♭7
Fmaj7
3
E♭7
D7

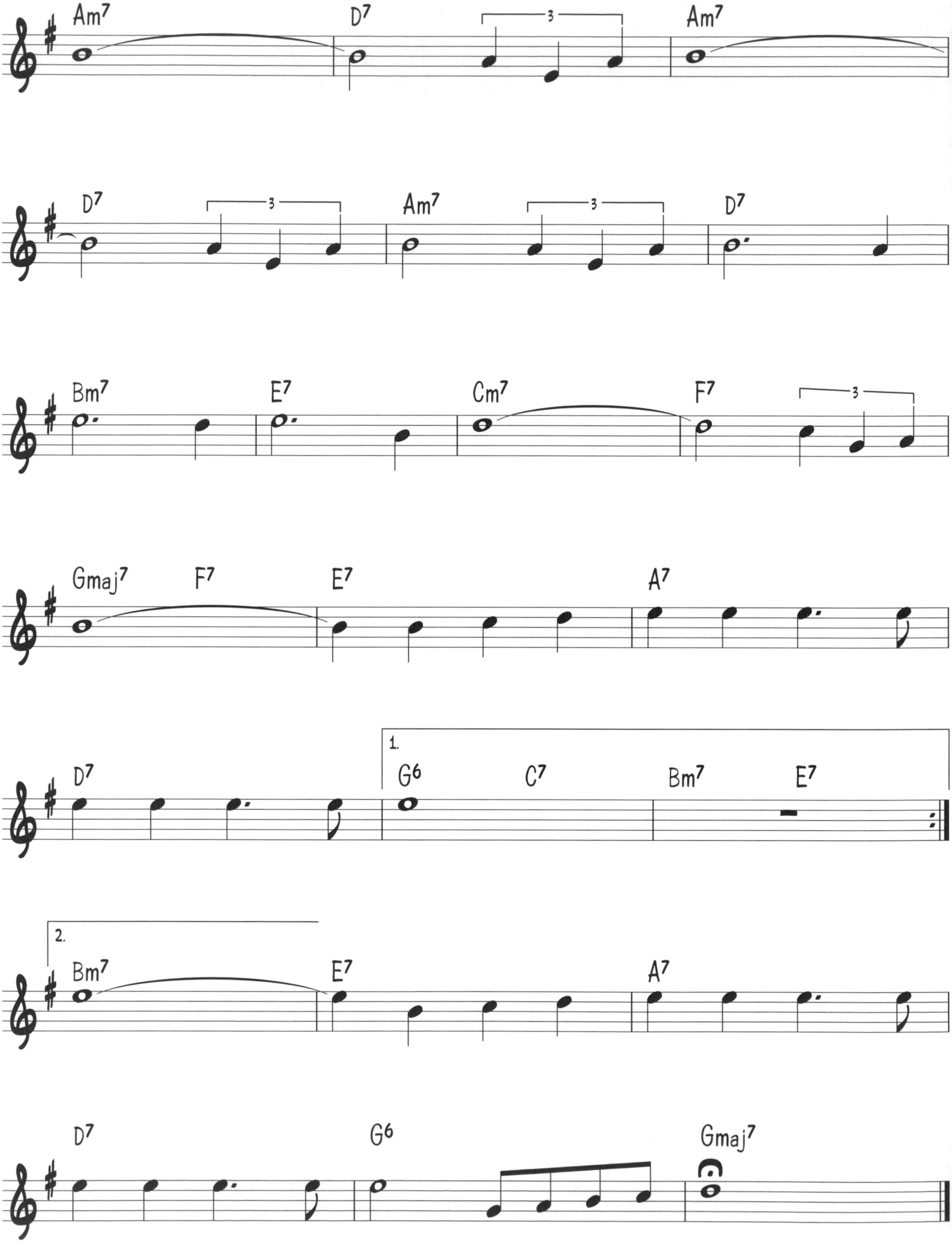
Am7 D7 3 Am7
D7 3 Am7 3 D7
Bm7 E7 Cm7 F7 3
Gmaj7 F7 E7 A7
D7 1. G6 C7 Bm7 E7
2. Bm7 E7 A7
D7 G6 Gmaj7

THE WAY YOU LOOK TONIGHT

FROM SWING TIME

Bb VERSION

WORDS BY DOROTHY FIELDS
MUSIC BY JEROME KERN

* SKIP CUE NOTES ON THE SOLOS.

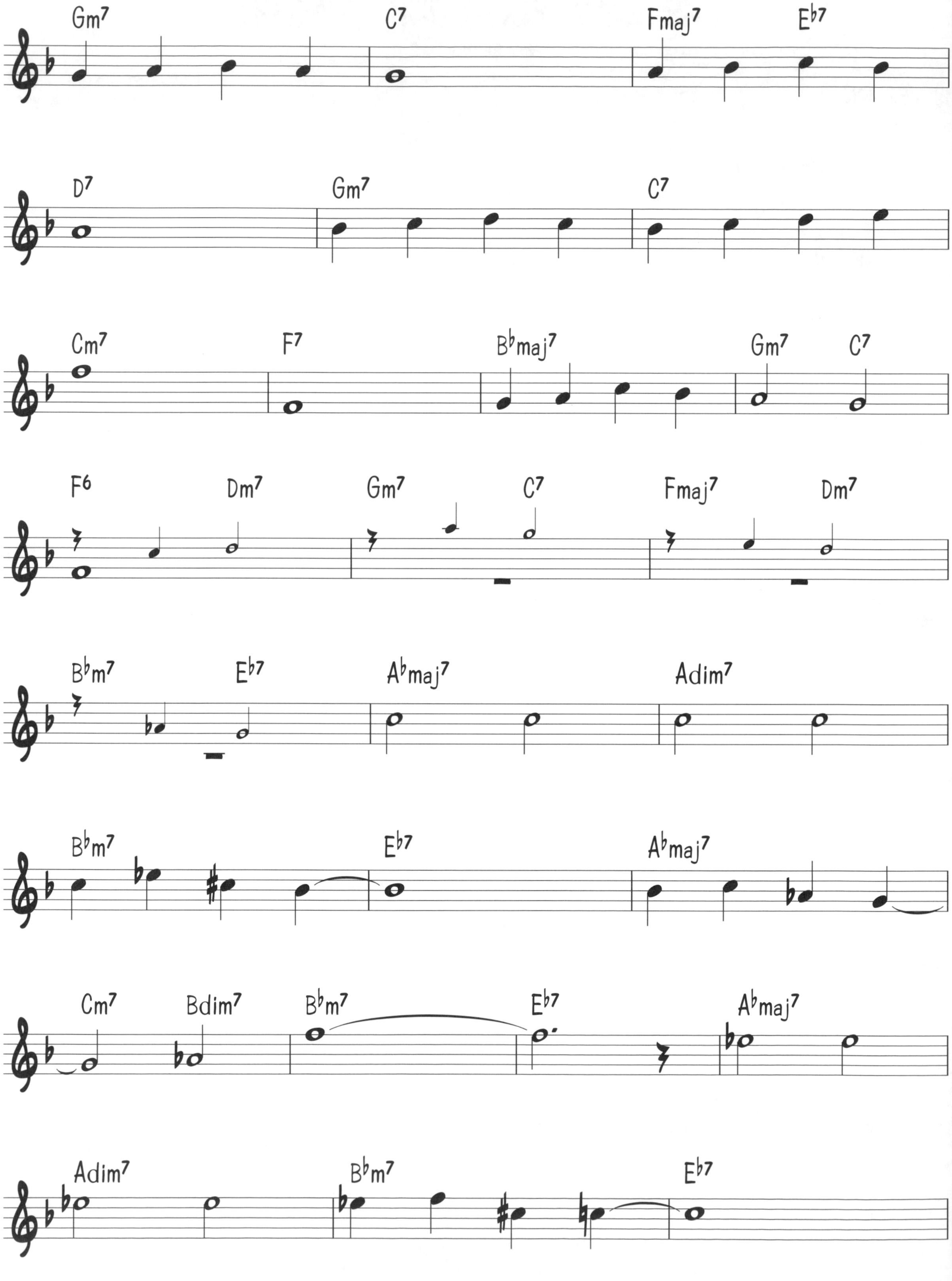
Gm7
C7
Fmaj7
E♭7
D7
Gm7
C7
Cm7
F7
B♭maj7
Gm7
C7
F6
Dm7
Gm7
C7
Fmaj7
Dm7
B♭m7
E♭7
A♭maj7
Adim7
B♭m7
E♭7
A♭maj7
Cm7
Bdim7
B♭m7
E♭7
A♭maj7
Adim7
B♭m7
E♭7

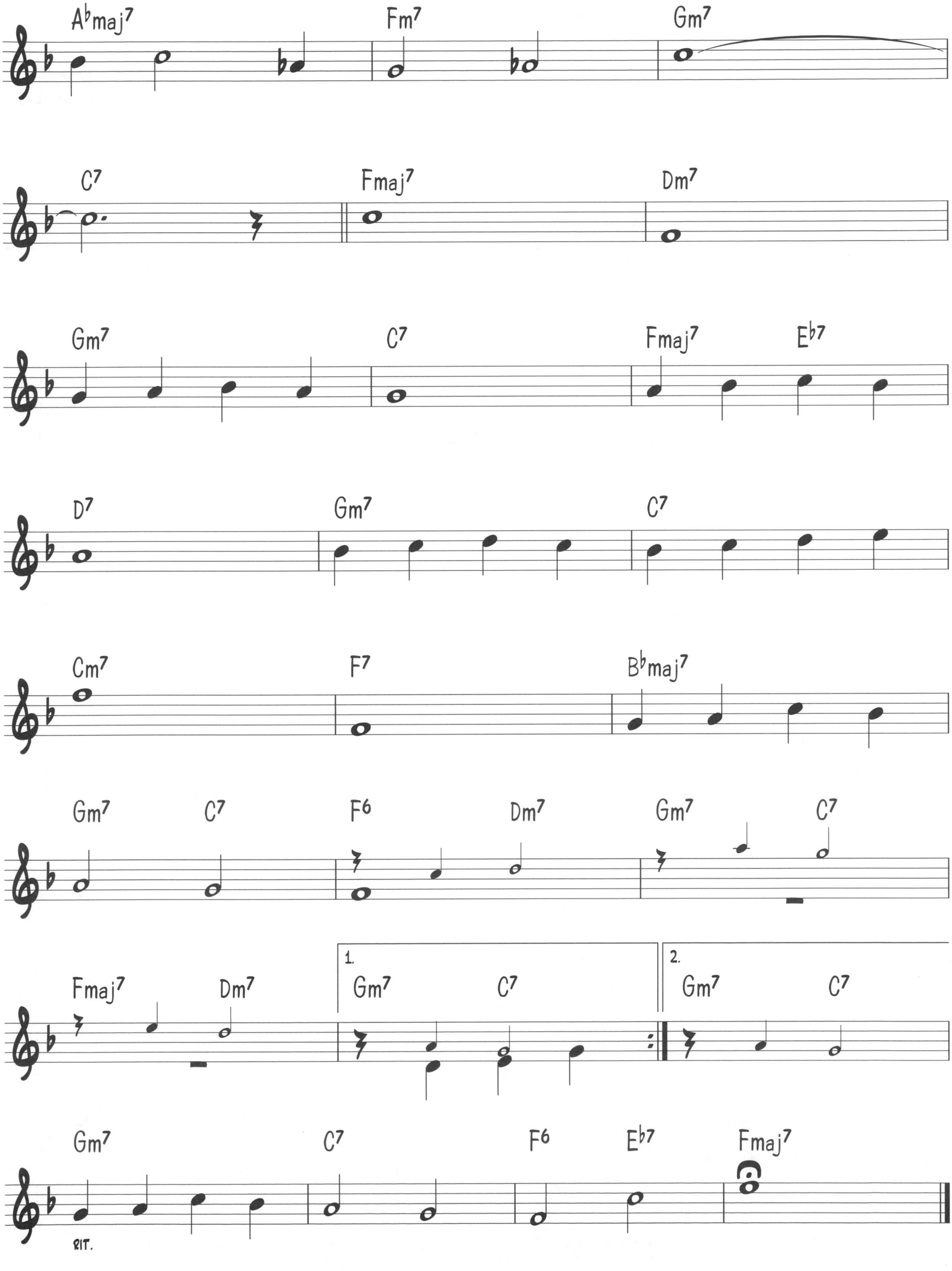
A♭maj7 Fm7 Gm7
C7 Fmaj7 Dm7
Gm7 C7 Fmaj7 E♭7
D7 Gm7 C7
Cm7 F7 B♭maj7
Gm7 C7 F6 Dm7 Gm7 C7
Fmaj7 Dm7 1. Gm7 C7 2. Gm7 C7
Gm7 C7 F6 E♭7 Fmaj7
RIT.

THE VERY THOUGHT OF YOU

B♭ VERSION

WORDS AND MUSIC BY
RAY NOBLE

Dm7 Cm7 F7 B♭maj7 E♭maj7 Dm7 Cm7 F7
B♭6 Cm7 C♯dim7 B♭6/D C7
3
Bdim7 Cm7 F7 Am7♭5 D7
Gm7 Em7♭5 Bdim7
Cm7 Bdim7 Cm7 F7
1.
B♭6 C♯7 Cm7 F7
2.
B♭6 Bmaj7 B♭maj7

WATCH WHAT HAPPENS

FROM THE UMBRELLAS OF CHERBOURG

B♭ VERSION

MUSIC BY MICHEL LEGRAND
ORIGINAL FRENCH TEXT BY JACQUES DEMY
ENGLISH LYRICS BY NORMAN GIMBEL

MEDIUM LATIN

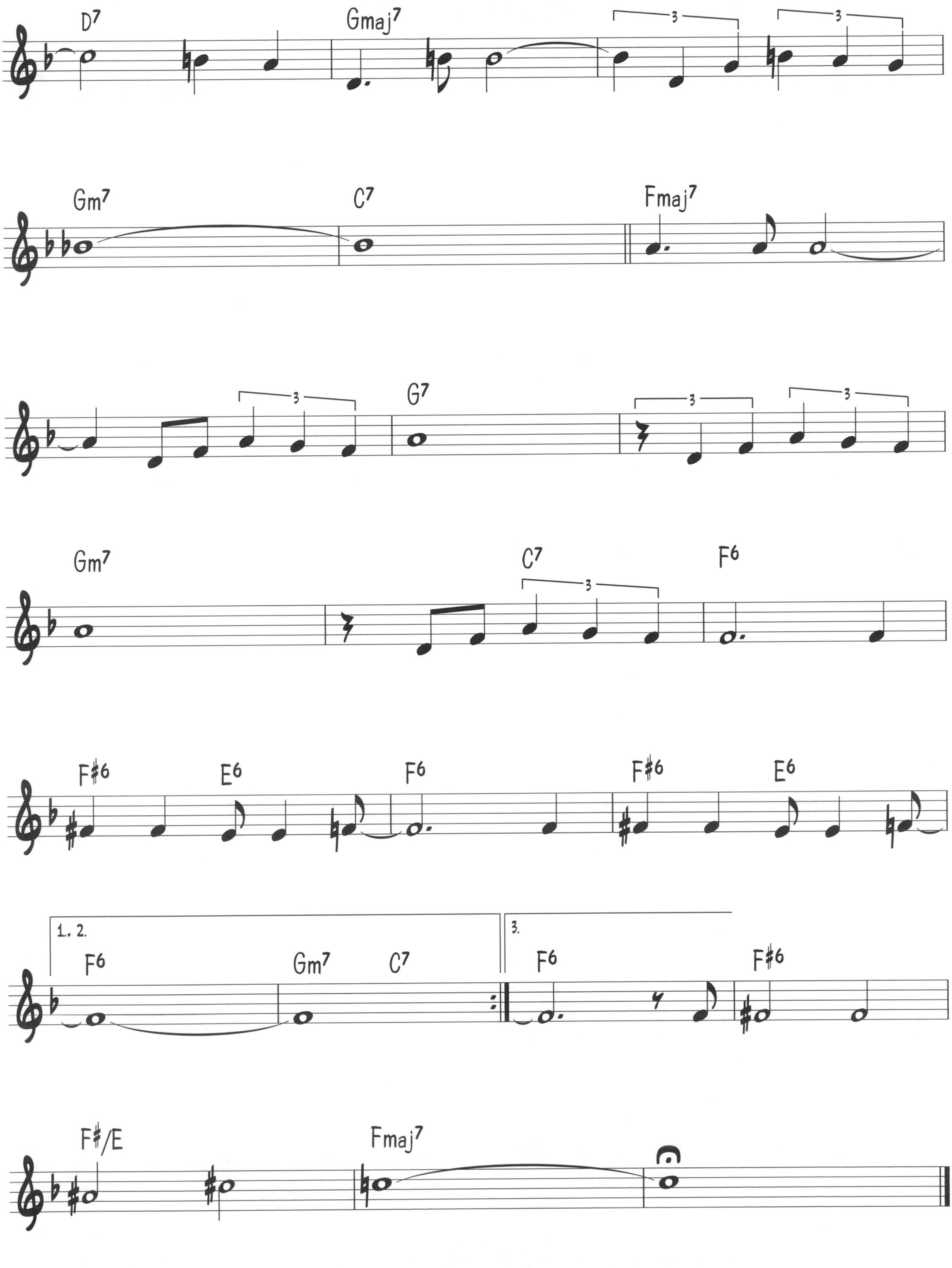
D7
Gmaj7
3
3
Gm7
C7
Fmaj7
3
G7
3
3
Gm7
C7
3
F6
F#6
E6
F6
F#6
E6
1., 2.
F6
Gm7
C7
3.
F6
F#6
F#/E
Fmaj7

YESTERDAYS

FROM ROBERTA

B♭ VERSION

WORDS BY OTTO HARBACH
MUSIC BY JEROME KERN

E^b Instruments

DON'T GET AROUND MUCH ANYMORE

FROM SOPHISTICATED LADY

E♭ VERSION

WORDS AND MUSIC BY DUKE ELLINGTON
AND BOB RUSSELL

* PLAY CUE NOTES FIRST AND LAST TIMES ONLY.

G7
Amaj7
A7
D6
D#m7
G#7
C#m7
Cdim7
Bm7
Amaj7
F#7
B7
E7
1.–3.
A6
C7
Bm7
E7
4.
A6
E7
A6
E7
A6
F7
E7
A6

EXACTLY LIKE YOU

E♭ VERSION

WORDS BY DOROTHY FIELDS
MUSIC BY JIMMY McHUGH

A7
D6
G7
A6
F♯m7
Bm7
Dm6
A6
Cdim7
Bm7
E7
A6
B7
Bm7
E7
1., 2.
A6
Bm7
E7
3.
A6
C6
B♭maj7
Amaj7

FLY ME TO THE MOON
(IN OTHER WORDS)

E♭ VERSION

WORDS AND MUSIC BY
BART HOWARD

E7
Amaj7
Dmaj7
G#m7b5
C#7
F#m7
A#dim7
Bm7
E7
C#7
F#7
TO CODA
1.
Bm7
A6
SOLO BREAK
2.
Bm7
E7
D.S. AL CODA
CODA
A6
G#m7b5
C#7
Bm7
A6
Bbmaj7
Amaj7

HAVE YOU MET MISS JONES?

FROM I'D RATHER BE RIGHT

Eb VERSION

WORDS BY LORENZ HART
MUSIC BY RICHARD RODGERS

D7
Gmaj7
Fm7
B♭7
E♭maj7
C♯m7
F♯7
Bmaj7
Fm7
B♭7
E♭maj7
Em7
A7
Dmaj7
F♯m7♭5
B7
Em7
A7
G7
F♯m7
B7
Em7
A7
D6
1.–4.
SOLO BREAK (1ST TIME)
Em7
A7
5.
Dmaj7

HONEYSUCKLE ROSE

FROM AIN'T MISBEHAVIN'

WORDS BY ANDY RAZAF
MUSIC BY THOMAS "FATS" WALLER

E♭ VERSION

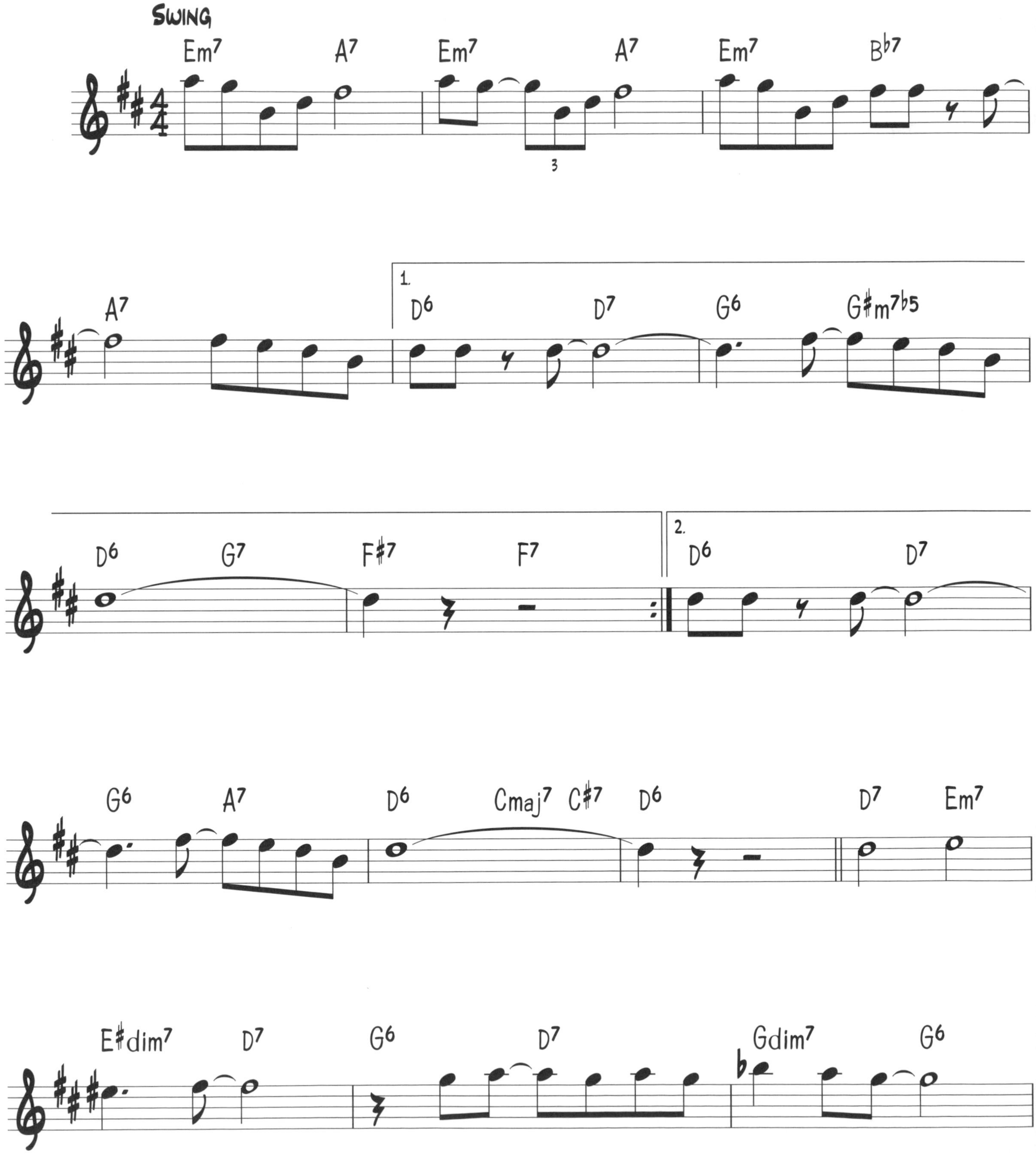

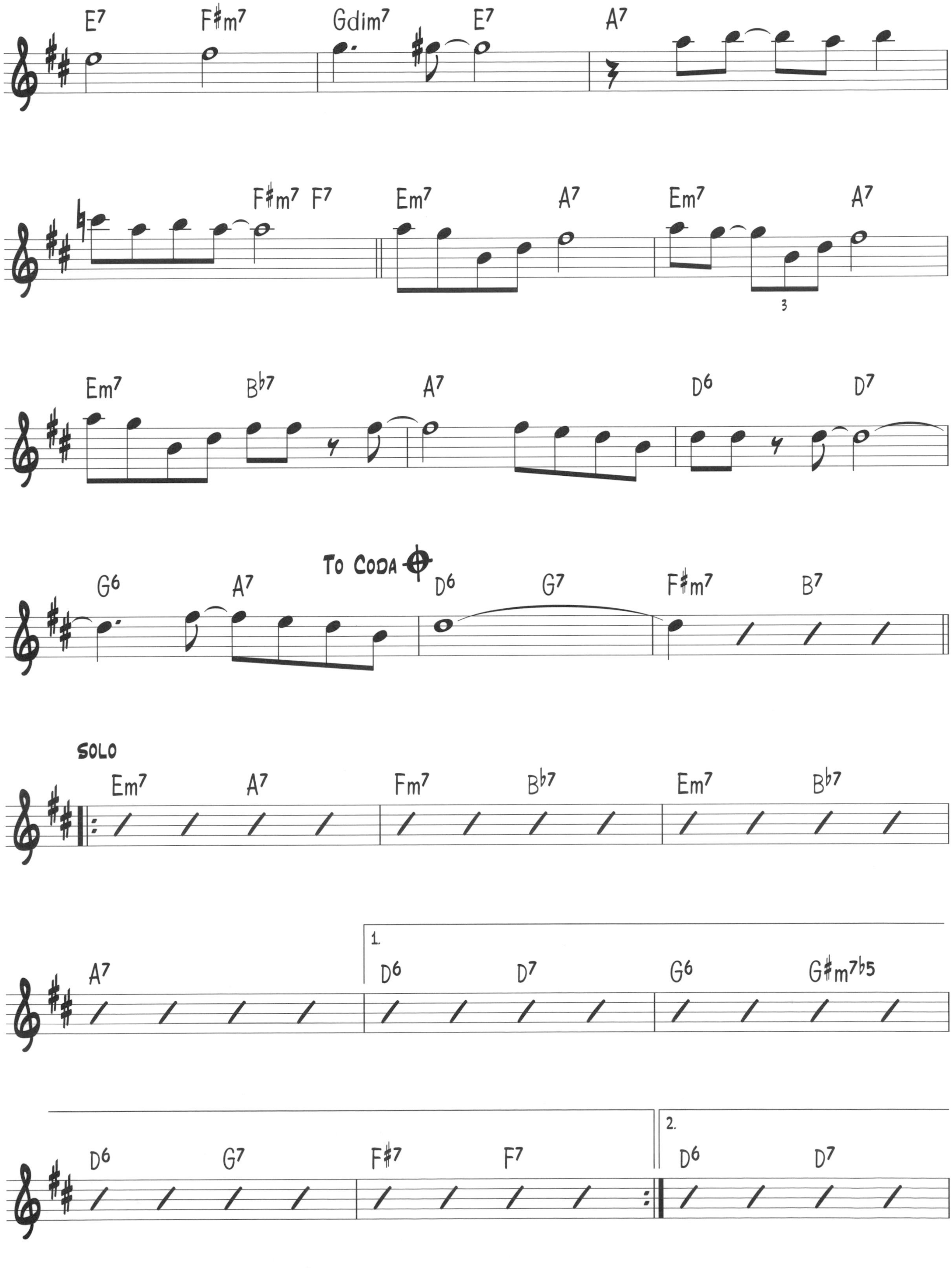
E7 F#m7 Gdim7 E7 A7
F#m7 F7 Em7 A7 Em7 A7
3
Em7 Bb7 A7 D6 D7
To Coda
G6 A7 D6 G7 F#m7 B7
SOLO
Em7 A7 Fm7 Bb7 Em7 Bb7
1.
A7 D6 D7 G6 G#m7b5
2.
D6 G7 F#7 F7 D6 D7

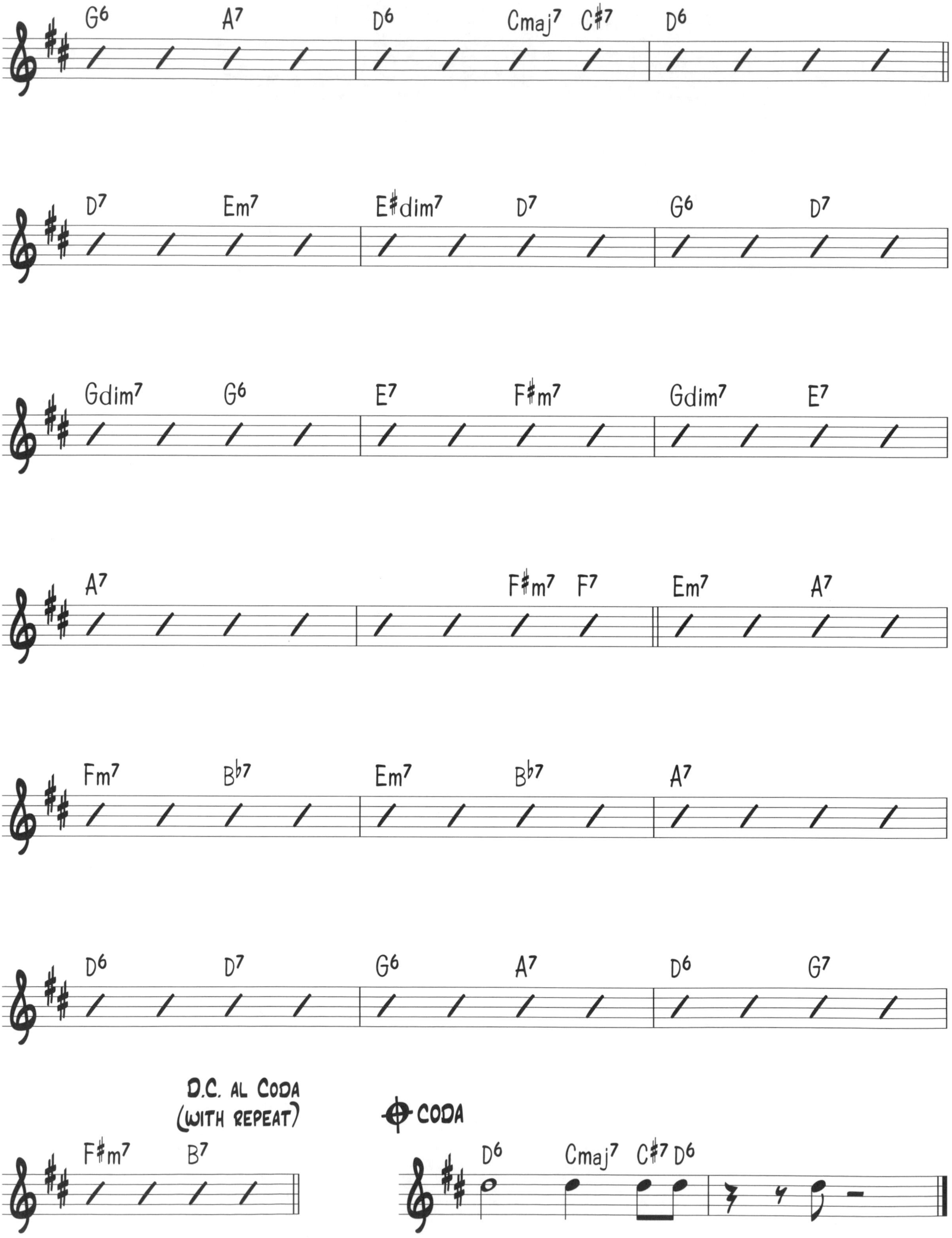
G6 A7 D6 Cmaj7 C#7 D6
D7 Em7 E#dim7 D7 G6 D7
Gdim7 G6 E7 F#m7 Gdim7 E7
A7 F#m7 F7 Em7 A7
Fm7 Bb7 Em7 Bb7 A7
D6 D7 G6 A7 D6 G7
D.C. al Coda
(with repeat)
F#m7 B7
CODA
D6 Cmaj7 C#7 D6

MY FAVORITE THINGS

FROM THE SOUND OF MUSIC

LYRICS BY OSCAR HAMMERSTEIN II
MUSIC BY RICHARD RODGERS

E♭ VERSION

INTRODUCTION
MEDIUM JAZZ WALTZ

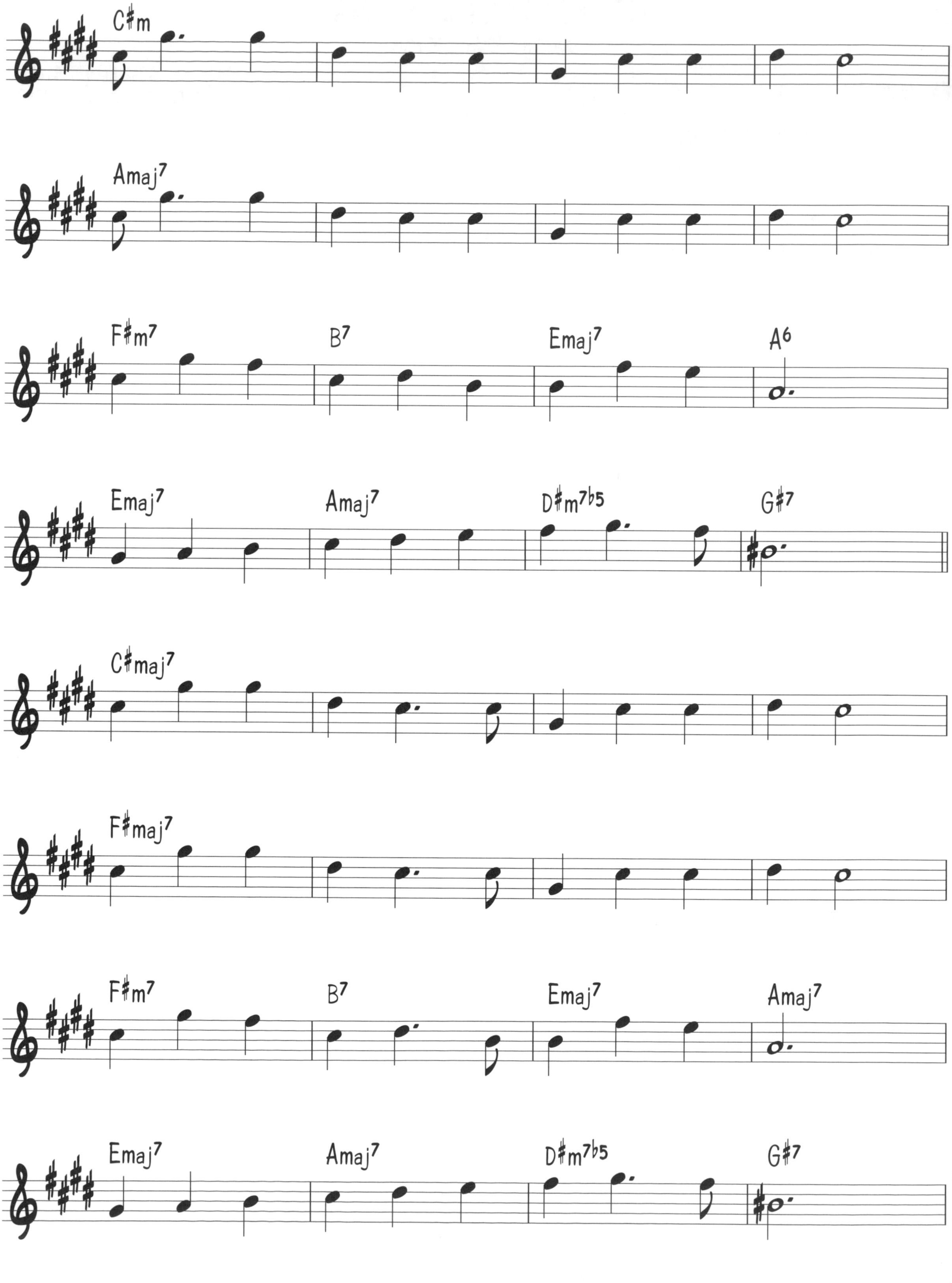
C#m
Amaj7
F#m7
B7
Emaj7
A6
Emaj7
Amaj7
D#m7b5
G#7
C#maj7
F#maj7
F#m7
B7
Emaj7
Amaj7
Emaj7
Amaj7
D#m7b5
G#7

C#m7
D#m7b5
G#7
C#m7
Amaj7
F#7
Emaj7
G7
F#m7
B7
1., 2.
Emaj7
Amaj7/E
Emaj7
Amaj7/E
Emaj7
Amaj7/E
D#m7b5
G#7
3.
Emaj7
Amaj7/E
Emaj7
Amaj7/E
Play 3 times
Emaj7
Amaj7/E
D#m7b5
G#7
C#m7

I REMEMBER YOU

FROM THE PARAMOUNT PICTURE THE FLEET'S IN

E♭ VERSION

WORDS BY JOHNNY MERCER
MUSIC BY VICTOR SCHERTZINGER

C#m7 F#7 Bmaj7 Bm7 E7
Amaj7 Fdim7 Em6 A7 Dmaj7 G#m7 C#7
Dmaj7 G7 F#m7 B7 Em7
C7 D6 G#m7b5 G7
1., 2.
F#m7 F7 Em7 A7 D6
SOLO BREAK (1ST TIME)
3.
F#m7 F7 Em7 A7 Fmaj7 D7 Gm7 C7
F#m7 F7 Em7 A7 D6 E/D

IF I SHOULD LOSE YOU

FROM THE PARAMOUNT PICTURE ROSE OF THE RANCHO

Eb VERSION

WORDS AND MUSIC BY LEO ROBIN
AND RALPH RAINGER

INTRODUCTION
MEDIUM LATIN

B7 F7 D#dim7/E Em7 F#m7 B7
D#dim7/E Em7 Dm7 G7 B/C Cmaj7
Dm7 G7 G7/C Cmaj7 G/B
Am7 D7 Gdim7 Gmaj7
B7 Em7 Am7 D7
1., 2. G6 F#m7b5 B7
3. G#maj7
Gmaj7

IT COULD HAPPEN TO YOU

FROM THE PARAMOUNT PICTURE AND THE ANGELS SING

E♭ VERSION

WORDS BY JOHNNY BURKE
MUSIC BY JAMES VAN HEUSEN

Em7 G#m7b5 C#7 Dmaj7
G7 F#7 B7 Em7
C7 Dmaj7 G7 F#m7b5 B7
Em7 A7 1., 2. D6 B9 Em7
A7 3. D6 B7 Em A7 F#m7
F7 Em7 A7 F#m7 B7 Em7
A7 Ebmaj7 Dmaj7

MOON RIVER

FROM THE PARAMOUNT PICTURE *BREAKFAST AT TIFFANY'S*

E♭ VERSION

WORDS BY JOHNNY MERCER
MUSIC BY HERNY MANCINI

INTRODUCTION
JAZZ WALTZ

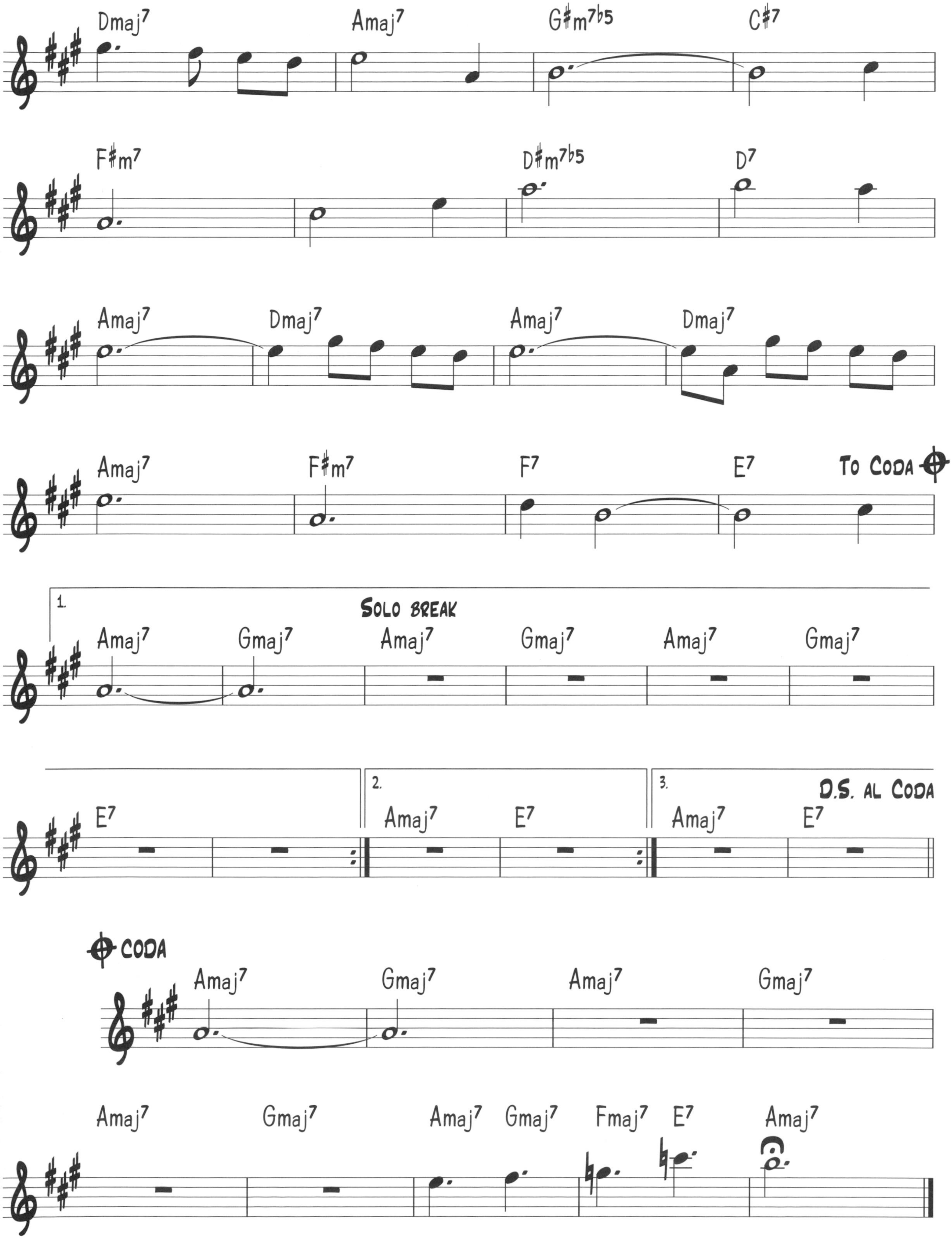
Dmaj7 Amaj7 G#m7b5 C#7
F#m7 D#m7b5 D7
Amaj7 Dmaj7 Amaj7 Dmaj7
Amaj7 F#m7 F7 E7
To Coda
1.
Solo break
Amaj7 Gmaj7 Amaj7 Gmaj7 Amaj7 Gmaj7
E7
2.
Amaj7 E7
3.
D.S. al Coda
Amaj7 E7
Coda
Amaj7 Gmaj7 Amaj7 Gmaj7
Amaj7 Gmaj7 Amaj7 Gmaj7 Fmaj7 E7 Amaj7

ON A SLOW BOAT TO CHINA

Eb VERSION

BY FRANK LOESSER

INTRODUCTION
MEDIUM SHUFFLE

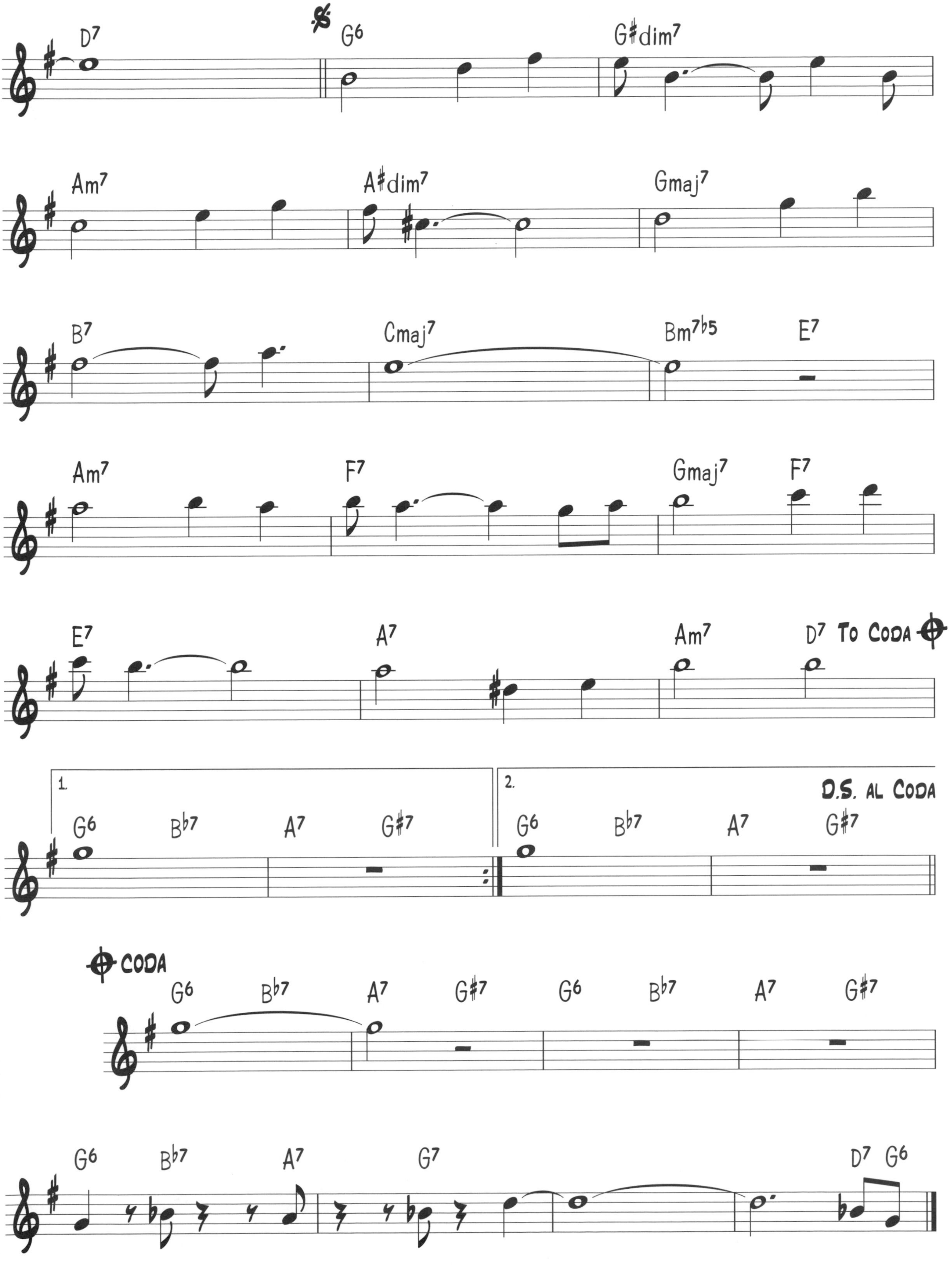
D7
G6
G#dim7
Am7
A#dim7
Gmaj7
B7
Cmaj7
Bm7b5
E7
Am7
F7
Gmaj7
F7
E7
A7
Am7
D7 To Coda
1.
2.
D.S. al Coda
G6 Bb7 A7 G#7
G6 Bb7 A7 G#7
Coda
G6 Bb7 A7 G#7 G6 Bb7 A7 G#7
G6 Bb7 A7 G7
D7 G6

OUT OF NOWHERE

FROM THE PARAMOUNT PICTURE DUDE RANCH

E♭ VERSION

WORDS BY EDWARD HEYMAN
MUSIC BY JOHNNY GREEN

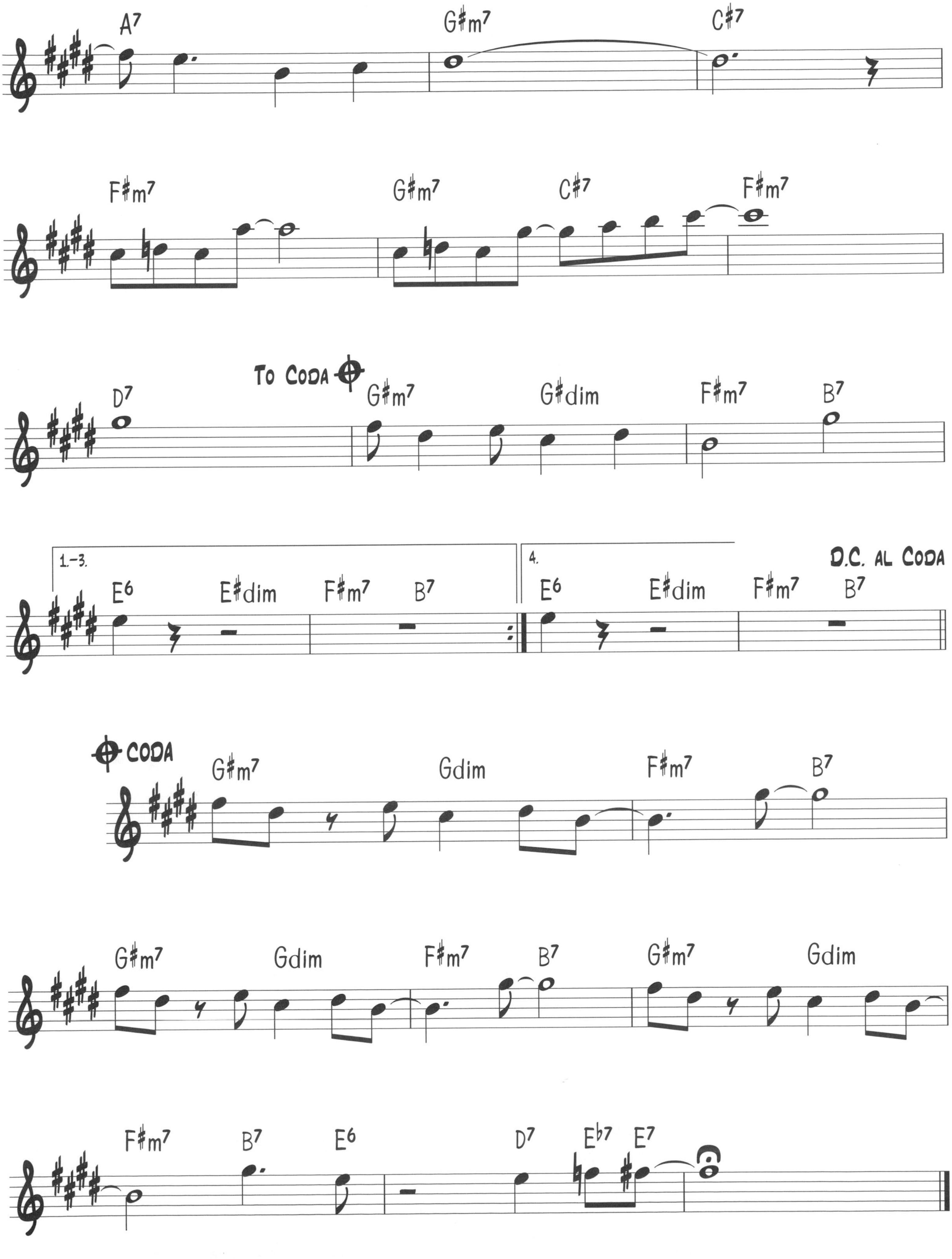
A7
G#m7
C#7
F#m7
G#m7
C#7
F#m7
TO CODA
D7
G#m7
G#dim
F#m7
B7
1.–3.
E6
E#dim
F#m7
B7
4.
E6
E#dim
F#m7
B7
D.C. AL CODA
CODA
G#m7
Gdim
F#m7
B7
G#m7
Gdim
F#m7
B7
G#m7
Gdim
F#m7
B7
E6
D7
Eb7
E7

SOFTLY AS IN A MORNING SUNRISE

FROM THE NEW MOON

E♭ VERSION

LYRICS BY OSCAR HAMMERSTEIN II
MUSIC BY SIGMUND ROMBERG

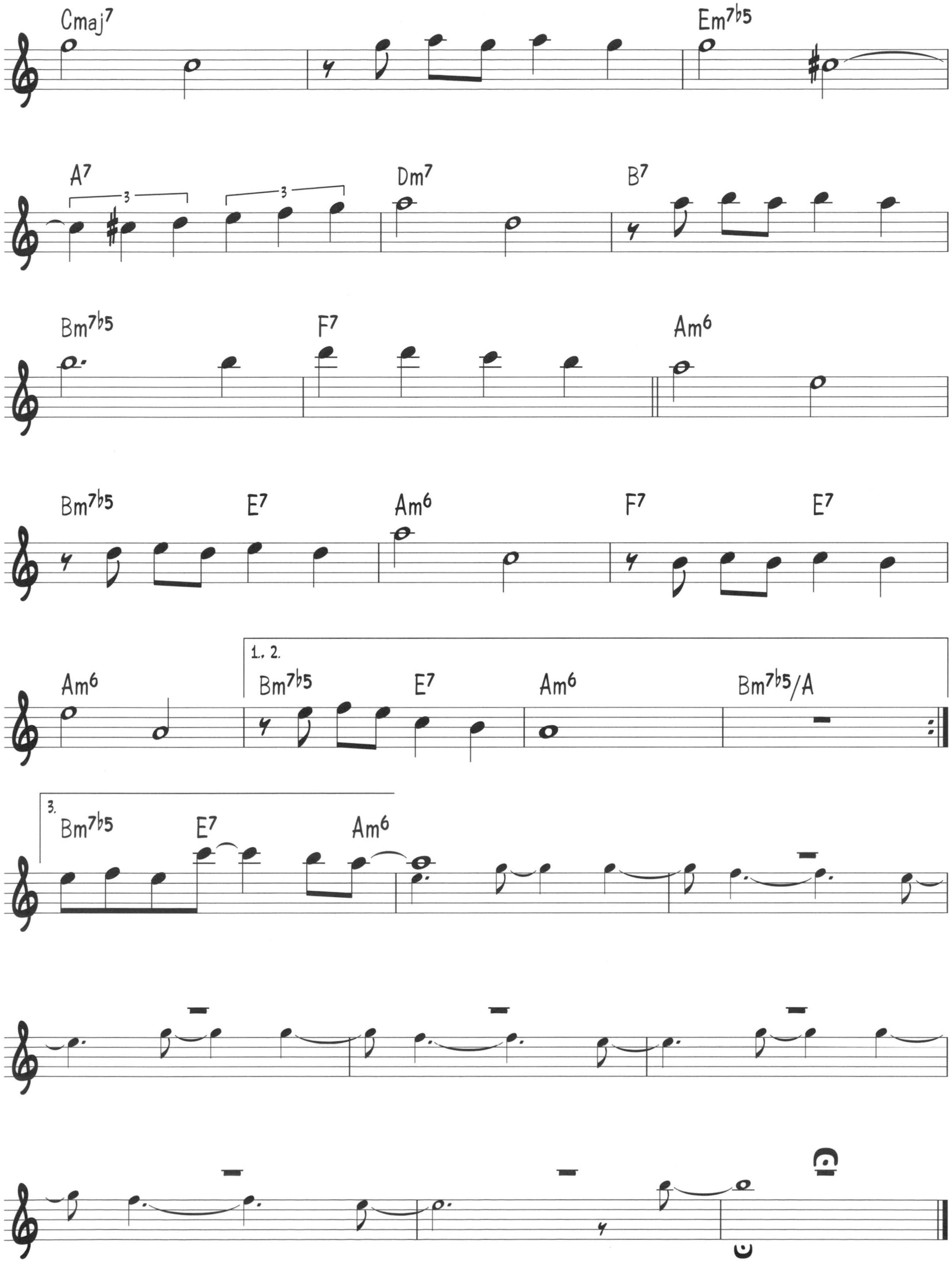
Cmaj7
Em7♭5
A7
3
3
Dm7
B7
Bm7♭5
F7
Am6
Bm7♭5
E7
Am6
F7
E7
Am6
1., 2.
Bm7♭5
E7
Am6
Bm7♭5/A
3.
Bm7♭5
E7
Am6

SPEAK LOW

FROM THE MUSICAL PRODUCTION ONE TOUCH OF VENUS

E♭ VERSION

WORDS BY OGDEN NASH
MUSIC BY KURT WEILL

Em7
A7
Em7
A7
F♯m7
B7
Gm7
C7
Gm7
C7
F♯m7
B7
Em7
A7
D6
Dm7
B♭7
Cmaj7
B♭7
A7

Em7
A7
3
Em7
A7
3
Em7
3
A7
F♯m7
B7
Gm7
C7
3
Dmaj7
C7
B7
E7
A7
1.
D6
G7
F♯m7
B7
2.
F♯m7
B7
E7
A7
D6
Dmaj7

THE WAY YOU LOOK TONIGHT

FROM SWING TIME

WORDS BY DOROTHY FIELDS
MUSIC BY JEROME KERN

E♭ VERSION

MEDIUM SWING

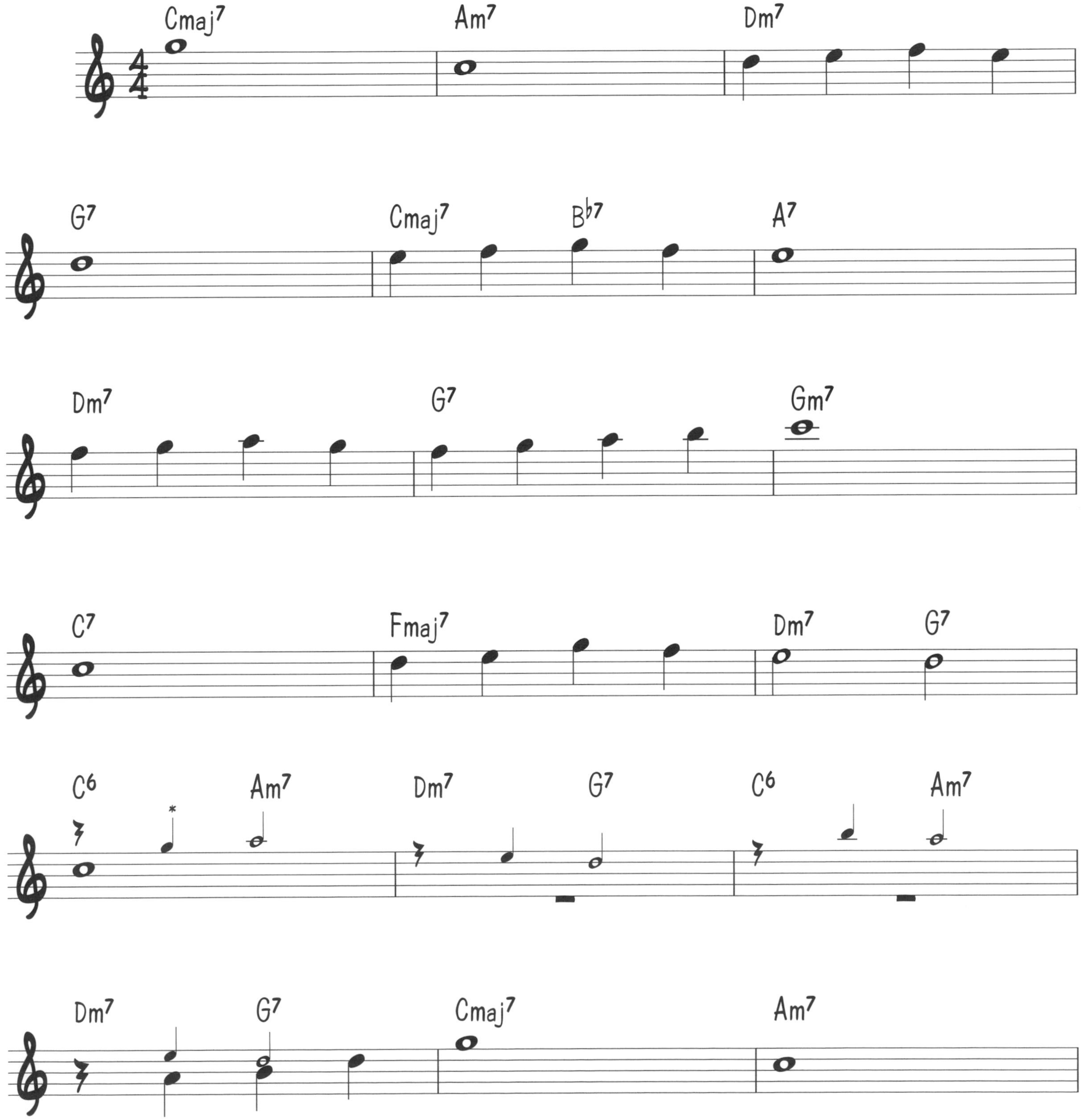

* SKIP CUE NOTES ON THE SOLOS.

Dm7
G7
Cmaj7
B♭7
A7
Dm7
G7
Gm7
C7
Fmaj7
Dm7
G7
C6
Am7
Dm7
G7
Cmaj7
Am7
Fm7
B♭7
E♭maj7
Edim7
Fm7
B♭7
E♭maj7
Gm7
F♯dim7
Fm7
B♭7
E♭maj7
Edim7
Fm7
B♭7

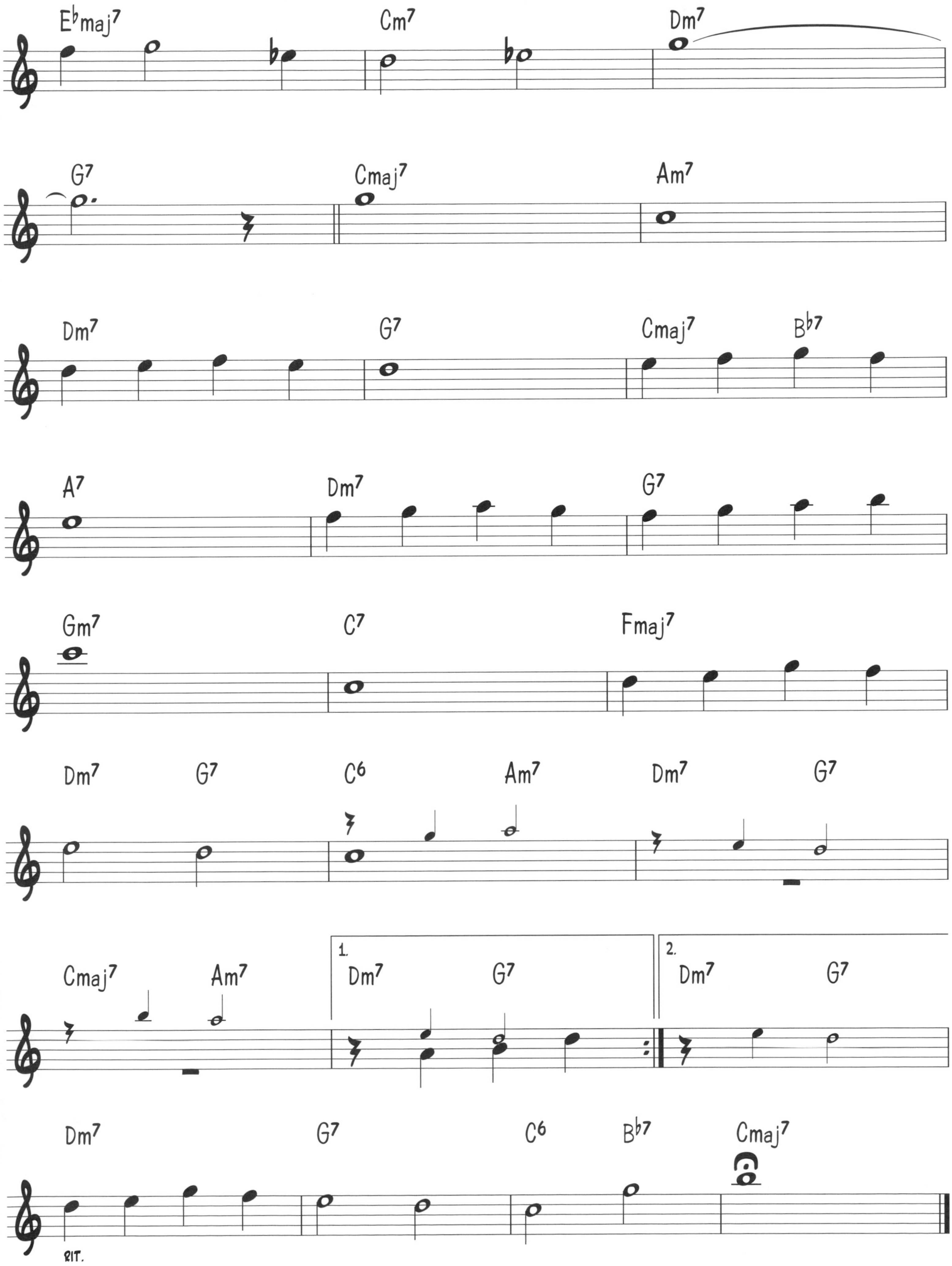
E♭maj7 Cm7 Dm7
G7 Cmaj7 Am7
Dm7 G7 Cmaj7 B♭7
A7 Dm7 G7
Gm7 C7 Fmaj7
Dm7 G7 C6 Am7 Dm7 G7
Cmaj7 Am7 1. Dm7 G7 2. Dm7 G7
Dm7 G7 C6 B♭7 Cmaj7
RIT.

THE VERY THOUGHT OF YOU

E♭ VERSION

WORDS AND MUSIC BY
RAY NOBLE

Am7 Gm7 C7 Fmaj7 B♭maj7 Am7 Gm7 C7
F6 Gm7 G♯dim7 F6/A G7
F♯dim7 Gm7 C7 Em7♭5 A7
Dm7 Bm7♭5 F♯dim7
Gm7 F♯dim7 Gm7 C7
1. F6 G♯7 Gm7 C7
2. F6 F♯maj7 Fmaj7

WATCH WHAT HAPPENS

FROM THE UMBRELLAS OF CHERBOURG

E♭ VERSION

MUSIC BY MICHEL LEGRAND
ORIGINAL FRENCH TEXT BY JACQUES DEMY
ENGLISH LYRICS BY NORMAN GIMBEL

MEDIUM LATIN

A7
Dmaj7
Dm7
G7
Cmaj7
D7
Dm7
G7
C6
C#6
B6
C6
C#6
B6
1., 2.
C6
Dm7
G7
3.
C6
C#6
C#/B
Cmaj7

YESTERDAYS

FROM ROBERTA

Eb VERSION

WORDS BY OTTO HARBACH
MUSIC BY JEROME KERN

C Bass Instruments

DON'T GET AROUND MUCH ANYMORE

FROM SOPHISTICATED LADY

𝄢 C VERSION

WORDS AND MUSIC BY DUKE ELLINGTON
AND BOB RUSSELL

* PLAY CUE NOTES FIRST AND LAST TIMES ONLY.

B♭7
Cmaj7
C7
F6
F♯m7
B7
Em7
E♭dim7
Dm7
Cmaj7
A7
D7
G7
1.–3.
C6
E♭7
Dm7
G7
4.
C6
G7
C6
G7
C6
A♭7
G7
C6

EXACTLY LIKE YOU

C VERSION

WORDS BY DOROTHY FIELDS
MUSIC BY JIMMY McHUGH

C7
F6
B♭7
C6
Am7
Dm7
Fm6
C6
E♭dim7
Dm7
G7
C6
D7
Dm7
G7
1., 2.
C6
Dm7
G7
3.
C6
E♭6
D♭maj7
Cmaj7

FLY ME TO THE MOON

(IN OTHER WORDS)

𝄢 C VERSION

WORDS AND MUSIC BY
BART HOWARD

G7
Cmaj7
Fmaj7
Bm7b5
E7
Am7
C#dim7
Dm7
G7
E7
A7
TO CODA
1.
Dm7
C6
SOLO BREAK
2.
Dm7
G7
C6
Bm7b5
E7
D.S. AL CODA
CODA
Dm7
C6
Dbmaj7
Cmaj7

HAVE YOU MET MISS JONES?

FROM I'D RATHER BE RIGHT

C VERSION

WORDS BY LORENZ HART
MUSIC BY RICHARD RODGERS

F7
B♭maj7
A♭m7
D♭7
G♭maj7
Em7
A7
Dmaj7
A♭m7
D♭7
G♭maj7
Gm7
C7
Fmaj7
Am7♭5
D7
Gm7
C7
B♭7
Am7
D7
Gm7
C7
F6
1.–4.
SOLO BREAK (1ST TIME)
Gm7
C7
5.
Fmaj7

HONEYSUCKLE ROSE

FROM AIN'T MISBEHAVIN'

C VERSION

WORDS BY ANDY RAZAF
MUSIC BY THOMAS "FATS" WALLER

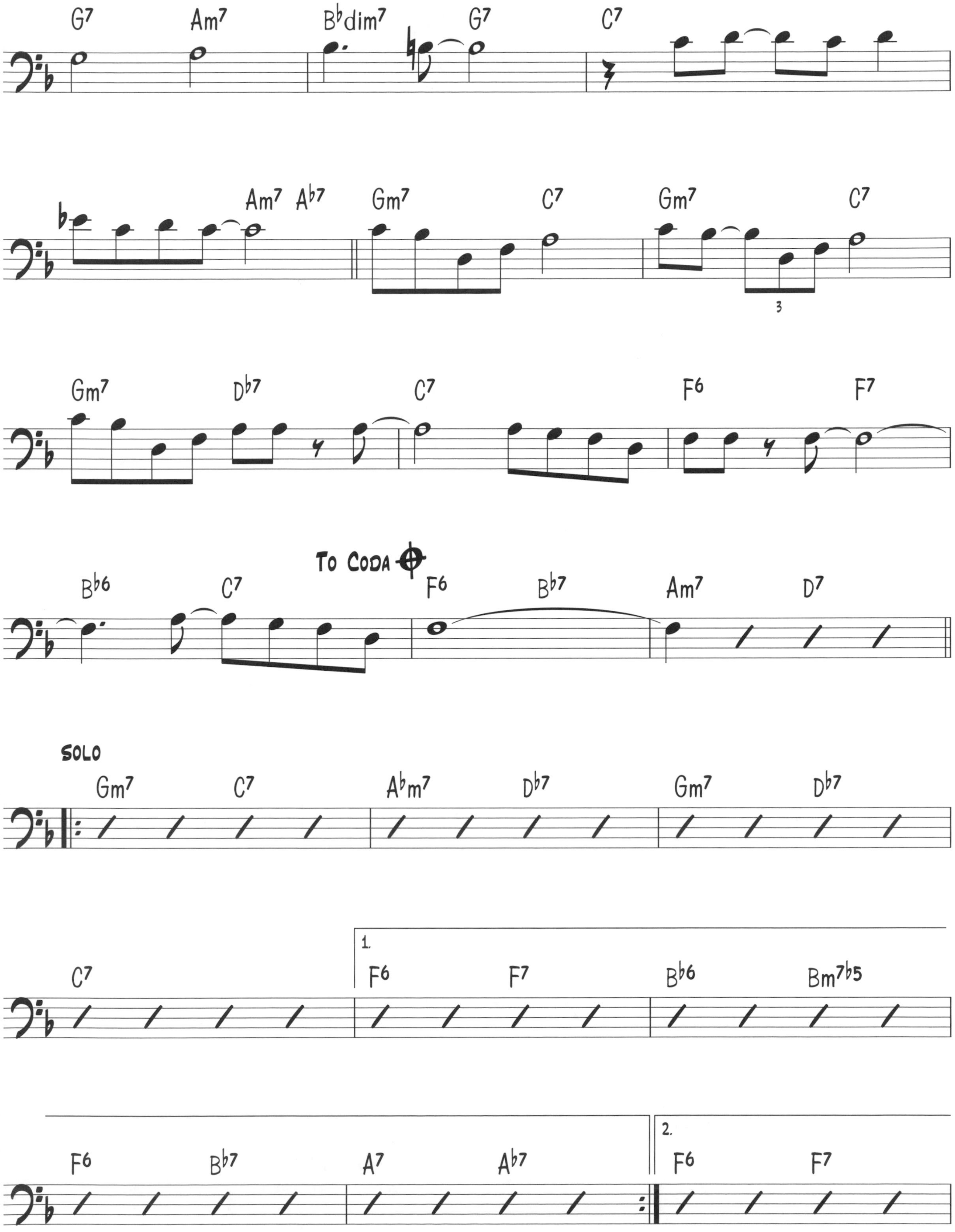
G7 Am7 B♭dim7 G7 C7
Am7 A♭7 Gm7 C7 Gm7 C7
3
Gm7 D♭7 C7 F6 F7
To Coda
B♭6 C7 F6 B♭7 Am7 D7
SOLO
Gm7 C7 A♭m7 D♭7 Gm7 D♭7
1.
C7 F6 F7 B♭6 Bm7♭5
2.
F6 B♭7 A7 A♭7 F6 F7

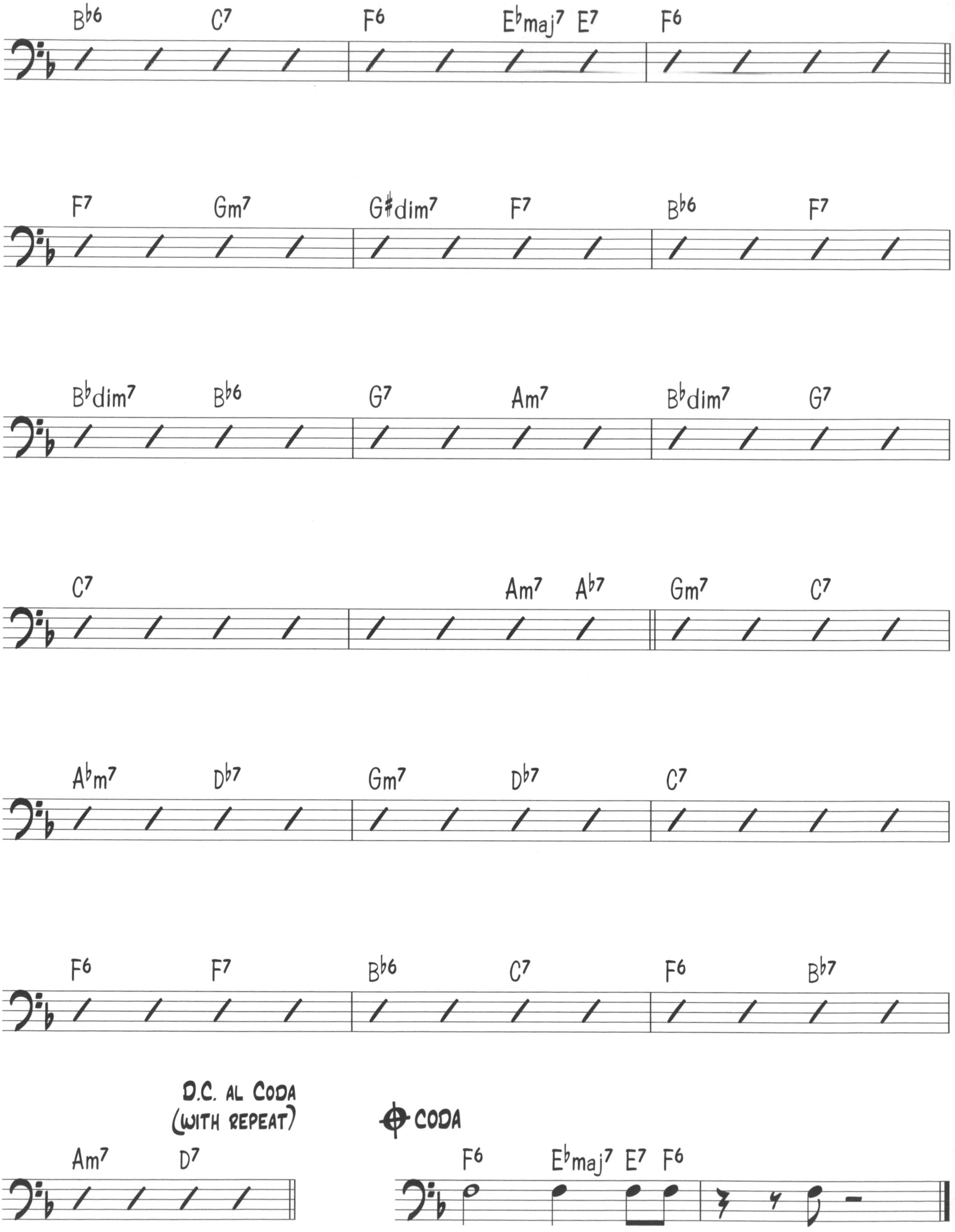
B♭6 C7 F6 E♭maj7 E7 F6
F7 Gm7 G♯dim7 F7 B♭6 F7
B♭dim7 B♭6 G7 Am7 B♭dim7 G7
C7 Am7 A♭7 Gm7 C7
A♭m7 D♭7 Gm7 D♭7 C7
F6 F7 B♭6 C7 F6 B♭7
D.C. al Coda
(with repeat)
Am7 D7
CODA
F6 E♭maj7 E7 F6

MY FAVORITE THINGS

FROM THE SOUND OF MUSIC

C VERSION

LYRICS BY OSCAR HAMMERSTEIN II
MUSIC BY RICHARD RODGERS

Em
Cmaj7
Am7
D7
Gmaj7
C6
Gmaj7
Cmaj7
F#m7b5
B7
Emaj7
Amaj7
Am7
D7
Gmaj7
Cmaj7
Gmaj7
Cmaj7
F#m7b5
B7

Em7
F#m7b5
B7
Em7
Cmaj7
A7
Gmaj7
Bb7
Am7
D7
1., 2.
Gmaj7
Cmaj7/G
Gmaj7
Cmaj7/G
Gmaj7
Cmaj7/G
F#m7b5
B7
3.
Gmaj7
Cmaj7/G
Gmaj7
Cmaj7/G
PLAY 3 TIMES
Gmaj7
Cmaj7/G
F#m7b5
B7
Em7

I REMEMBER YOU

FROM THE PARAMOUNT PICTURE THE FLEET'S IN

C VERSION

WORDS BY JOHNNY MERCER
MUSIC BY VICTOR SCHERTZINGER

Em7 A7 Dmaj7 Dm7 G7
Cmaj7 Ab dim7 Gm6 C7 Fmaj7 Bm7 E7
Fmaj7 Bb7 Am7 D7 Gm7
Eb7 F6 Bm7b5 Bb7
1., 2.
Am7 Ab7 Gm7 C7 F6
SOLO BREAK (1ST TIME)
3.
Am7 Ab7 Gm7 C7 Abmaj7 F7 Bbm7 Eb7
Am7 Ab7 Gm7 C7 F6 G/F

IF I SHOULD LOSE YOU

FROM THE PARAMOUNT PICTURE ROSE OF THE RANCHO

𝄢 C VERSION

WORDS AND MUSIC BY LEO ROBIN
AND RALPH RAINGER

INTRODUCTION
MEDIUM LATIN

D7
A♭7
F♯dim7/G
Gm7
Am7
D7
F♯dim7/G
Gm7
Fm7
B♭7
D/E♭
E♭maj7
Fm7
B♭7
B♭7/E♭
E♭maj7
B♭/D
Cm7
F7
B♭dim7
B♭maj7
D7
Gm7
Cm7
F7
1., 2.
B♭6
Am7♭5
D7
3.
Bmaj7
B♭maj7

IT COULD HAPPEN TO YOU

FROM THE PARAMOUNT PICTURE AND THE ANGELS SING

C VERSION

WORDS BY JOHNNY BURKE
MUSIC BY JAMES VAN HEUSEN

Gm7
Bm7b5
E7
Fmaj7
Bb7
A7
D7
Gm7
Eb7
Fmaj7
Bb7
Am7b5
D7
Gm7
C7
1., 2.
F6
D9
Gm7
C7
3.
F6
D7
Gm
C7
Am7
Ab7
Gm7
C7
Am7
D7
Gm7
C7
Gbmaj7
Fmaj7

MOON RIVER

from the Paramount Picture *BREAKFAST AT TIFFANY'S*

𝄢 C VERSION

Words by Johnny Mercer
Music by Herny Mancini

Fmaj7
Cmaj7
Bm7♭5
E7
Am7
F♯m7♭5
F7
Cmaj7
Fmaj7
Cmaj7
Fmaj7
Cmaj7
Am7
A♭7
G7
TO CODA
1.
SOLO BREAK
Cmaj7
B♭maj7
Cmaj7
B♭maj7
Cmaj7
B♭maj7
G7
2.
Cmaj7
G7
3.
D.S. AL CODA
Cmaj7
G7
CODA
Cmaj7
B♭maj7
Cmaj7
B♭maj7
Cmaj7
B♭maj7
Cmaj7
B♭maj7
A♭maj7
G7
Cmaj7

ON A SLOW BOAT TO CHINA

C VERSION

BY FRANK LOESSER

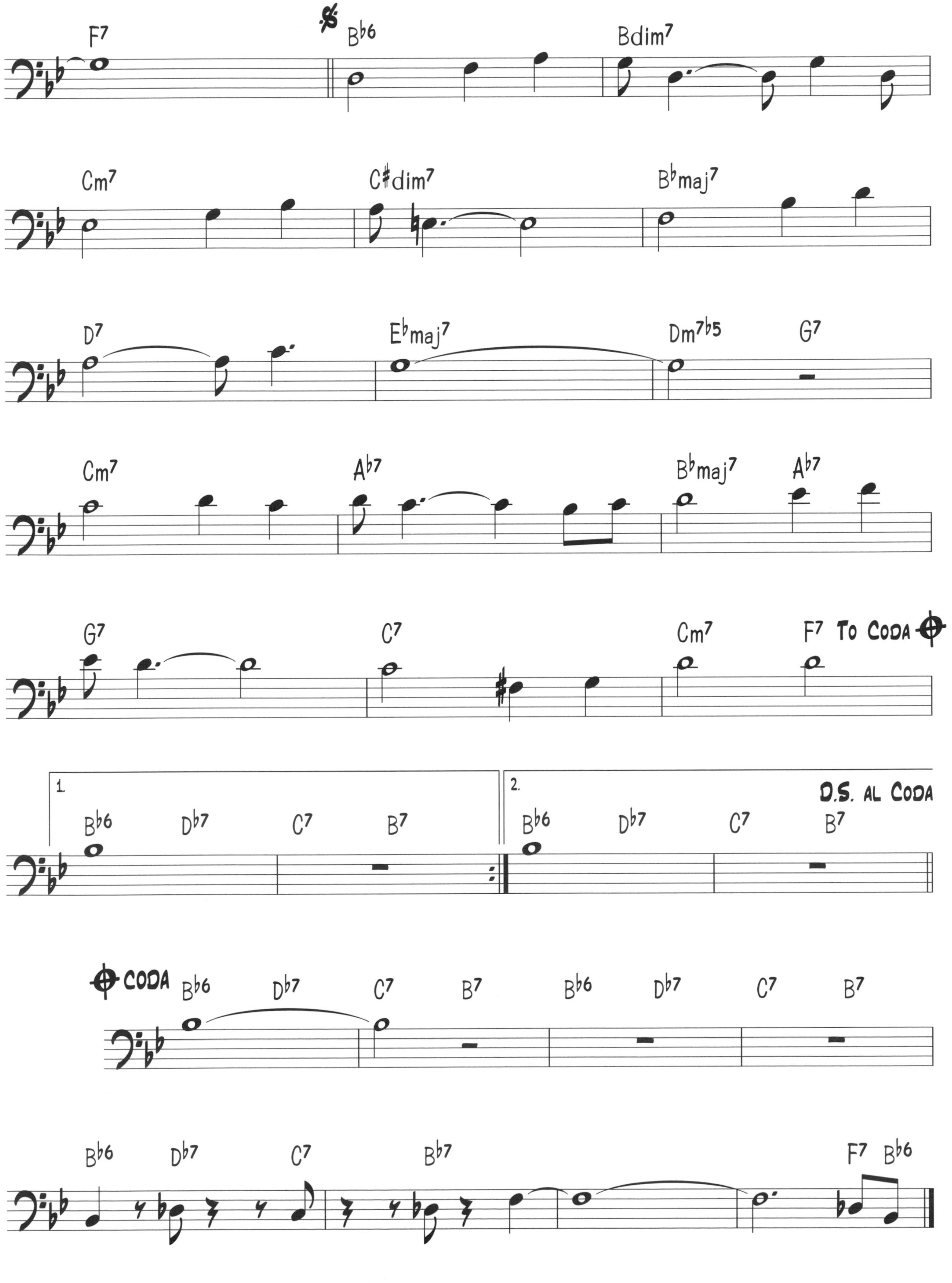
F7
Bb6 Bdim7
Cm7 C#dim7 Bbmaj7
D7 Ebmaj7 Dm7b5 G7
Cm7 Ab7 Bbmaj7 Ab7
G7 C7 Cm7 F7 To Coda
1. Bb6 Db7 C7 B7
2. D.S. al Coda
Bb6 Db7 C7 B7
Coda
Bb6 Db7 C7 B7 Bb6 Db7 C7 B7
Bb6 Db7 C7 Bb7 F7 Bb6

OUT OF NOWHERE

FROM THE PARAMOUNT PICTURE DUDE RANCH

𝄢 C VERSION

WORDS BY EDWARD HEYMAN
MUSIC BY JOHNNY GREEN

C7
Bm7
E7
Am7
Bm7
E7
Am7
To Coda
F7
Bm7
Bdim
Am7
D7
1.–3.
G6
G♯dim
Am7
D7
4.
D.C. al Coda
G6
G♯dim
Am7
D7
CODA
Bm7
B♭dim
Am7
D7
Bm7
B♭dim
Am7
D7
Bm7
B♭dim
Am7
D7
G6
F7
G♭7
G7

SOFTLY AS IN A MORNING SUNRISE

FROM THE NEW MOON

𝄢 C VERSION

LYRICS BY OSCAR HAMMERSTEIN II
MUSIC BY SIGMUND ROMBERG

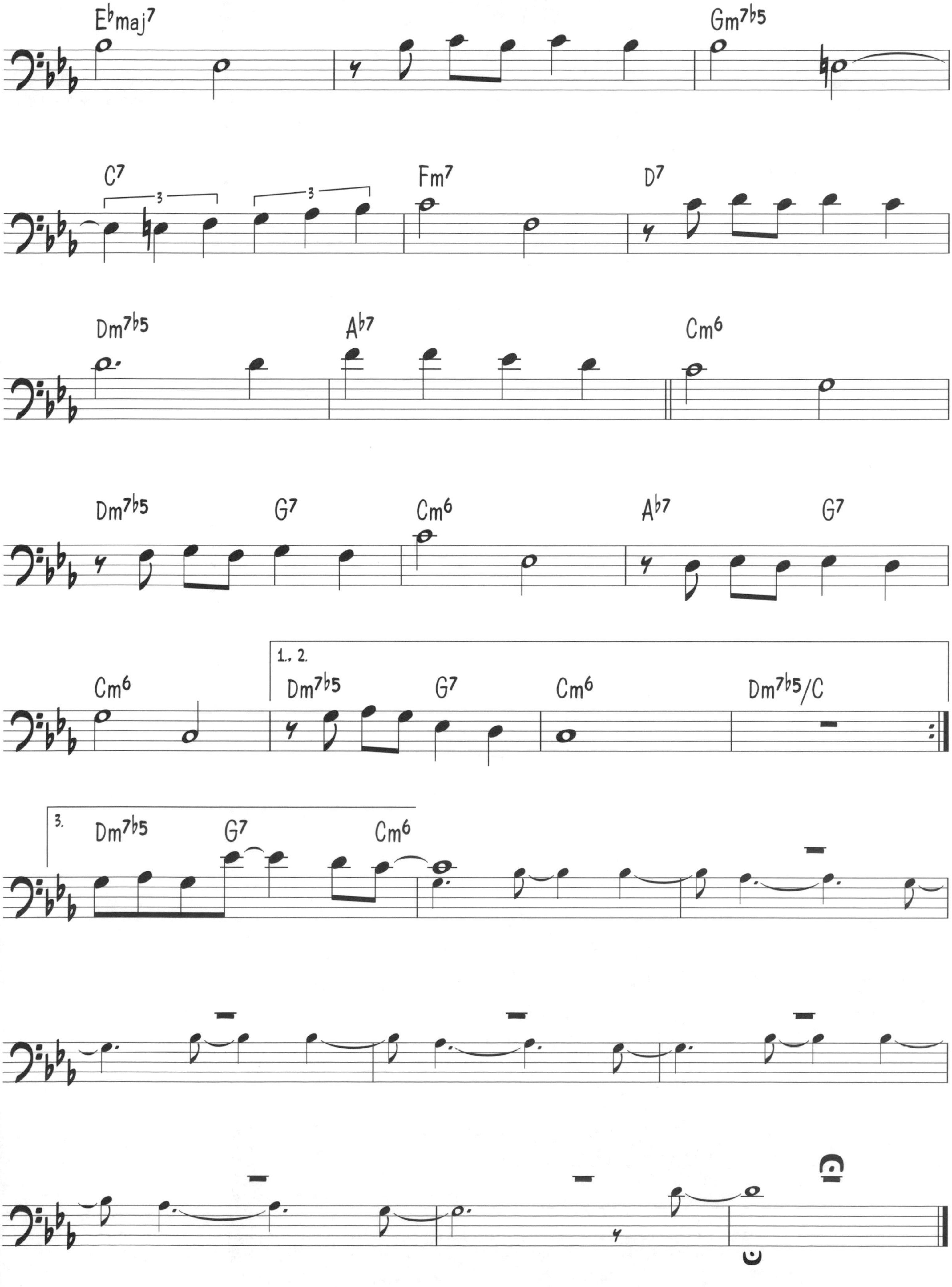
E♭maj7
Gm7♭5
C7
3
3
Fm7
D7
Dm7♭5
A♭7
Cm6
Dm7♭5
G7
Cm6
A♭7
G7
Cm6
1., 2.
Dm7♭5
G7
Cm6
Dm7♭5/C
3.
Dm7♭5
G7
Cm6

SPEAK LOW

FROM THE MUSICAL PRODUCTION ONE TOUCH OF VENUS

𝄢 C VERSION

WORDS BY OGDEN NASH
MUSIC BY KURT WEILL

Gm7 C7 Gm7
C7 Am7 D7
B♭m7 E♭7 B♭m7
E♭7 Am7 D7 Gm7 C7
F6 Fm7
D♭7 E♭maj7
D♭7 C7

Gm7
C7
3
Gm7
C7
3
Gm7
3
C7
Am7
D7
B♭m7
E♭7
3
Fmaj7
E♭7
D7
G7
C7
1.
F6
B♭7
Am7
D7
2.
Am7
D7
G7
C7
F6
Fmaj7

THE WAY YOU LOOK TONIGHT

FROM SWING TIME

𝄢 C VERSION

WORDS BY DOROTHY FIELDS
MUSIC BY JEROME KERN

MEDIUM SWING

* SKIP CUE NOTES ON THE SOLOS.

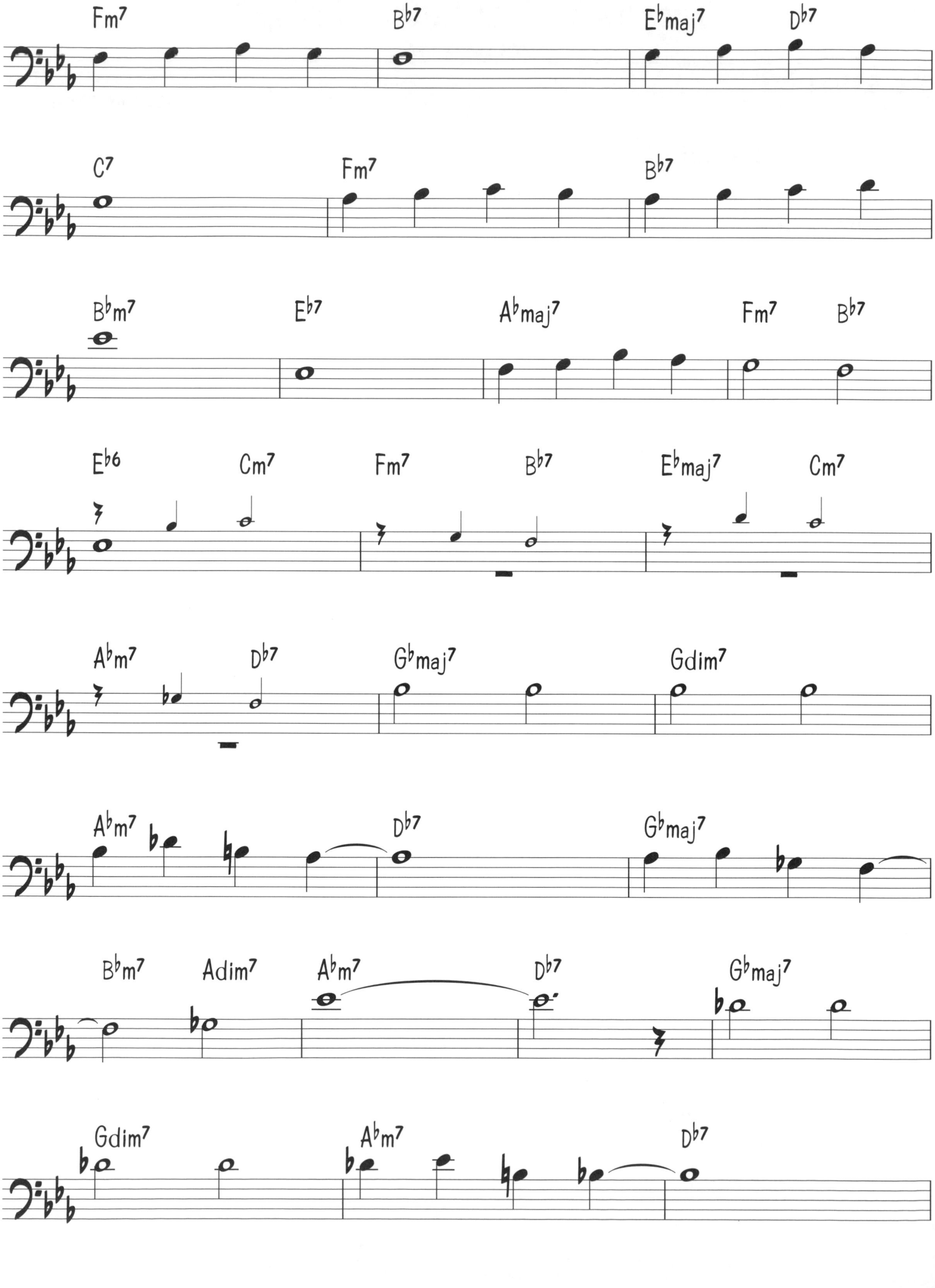
Fm7
B♭7
E♭maj7
D♭7
C7
Fm7
B♭7
B♭m7
E♭7
A♭maj7
Fm7
B♭7
E♭6
Cm7
Fm7
B♭7
E♭maj7
Cm7
A♭m7
D♭7
G♭maj7
Gdim7
A♭m7
D♭7
G♭maj7
B♭m7
Adim7
A♭m7
D♭7
G♭maj7
Gdim7
A♭m7
D♭7

Gbmaj7 Ebm7 Fm7
Bb7 Ebmaj7 Cm7
Fm7 Bb7 Ebmaj7 Db7
C7 Fm7 Bb7
Bbm7 Eb7 Abmaj7
Fm7 Bb7 Eb6 Cm7 Fm7 Bb7
Ebmaj7 Cm7
1.
Fm7 Bb7
2.
Fm7 Bb7
Fm7 Bb7 Eb6 Db7 Ebmaj7
RIT.

THE VERY THOUGHT OF YOU

C VERSION

WORDS AND MUSIC BY
RAY NOBLE

Cm7 B♭m7 E♭7 A♭maj7 D♭maj7 Cm7 B♭m7 E♭7
A♭6 B♭m7 Bdim7 A♭6/C B♭7
3
Adim7 B♭m7 E♭7 Gm7♭5 C7
Fm7 Dm7♭5 Adim7
B♭m7 Adim7 B♭m7 E♭7
1.
A♭6 B7 B♭m7 E♭7
2.
A♭6 Amaj7 A♭maj7

WATCH WHAT HAPPENS

FROM THE UMBRELLAS OF CHERBOURG

C VERSION

MUSIC BY MICHEL LEGRAND
ORIGINAL FRENCH TEXT BY JACQUES DEMY
ENGLISH LYRICS BY NORMAN GIMBEL

C7
Fmaj7
3
3
Fm7
B♭7
E♭maj7
3
F7
3
3
Fm7
B♭7
3
E♭6
E6
D6
E♭6
E6
D6
1., 2.
E♭6
Fm7
B♭7
3.
E♭6
E6
E/D
E♭maj7

YESTERDAYS

FROM ROBERTA

𝄢 C VERSION

WORDS BY OTTO HARBACH
MUSIC BY JEROME KERN

Presenting the Hal Leonard JAZZ PLAY-ALONG® SERIES

For use with all B-flat, E-flat, Bass Clef and C instruments, the Jazz Play-Along® Series is the ultimate learning tool for all jazz musicians. With musician-friendly lead sheets, melody cues, and other split-track choices on the included CD, these first-of-a-kind packages help you master improvisation while playing some of the greatest tunes of all time. FOR STUDY, each tune includes a split track with: melody cue with proper style and inflection • professional rhythm tracks • choruses for soloing • removable bass part • removable piano part. FOR PERFORMANCE, each tune also has: an additional full stereo accompaniment track (no melody) • additional choruses for soloing.

1. DUKE ELLINGTON
00841644 .... $16.95

1A. MAIDEN VOYAGE/ALL BLUES
00843158 .... $15.99

2. MILES DAVIS
00841645 .... $16.95

3. THE BLUES
00841646 .... $16.99

4. JAZZ BALLADS
00841691 .... $16.99

5. BEST OF BEBOP
00841689 .... $16.95

6. JAZZ CLASSICS WITH EASY CHANGES
00841690 .... $16.99

7. ESSENTIAL JAZZ STANDARDS
00843000 .... $16.99

8. ANTONIO CARLOS JOBIM AND THE ART OF THE BOSSA NOVA
00843001 .... $16.95

9. DIZZY GILLESPIE
00843002 .... $16.99

10. DISNEY CLASSICS
00843003 .... $16.99

11. RODGERS AND HART FAVORITES
00843004 .... $16.99

12. ESSENTIAL JAZZ CLASSICS
00843005 .... $16.99

13. JOHN COLTRANE
00843006 .... $16.95

14. IRVING BERLIN
00843007 .... $15.99

15. RODGERS & HAMMERSTEIN
00843008 .... $15.99

16. COLE PORTER
00843009 .... $15.95

17. COUNT BASIE
00843010 .... $16.95

18. HAROLD ARLEN
00843011 .... $15.95

19. COOL JAZZ
00843012 .... $15.95

20. CHRISTMAS CAROLS
00843080 .... $14.95

21. RODGERS AND HART CLASSICS
00843014 .... $14.95

22. WAYNE SHORTER
00843015 .... $16.95

23. LATIN JAZZ
00843016 .... $16.95

24. EARLY JAZZ STANDARDS
00843017 .... $14.95

25. CHRISTMAS JAZZ
00843018 .... $16.95

26. CHARLIE PARKER
00843019 .... $16.95

27. GREAT JAZZ STANDARDS
00843020 .... $16.99

28. BIG BAND ERA
00843021 .... $15.99

29. LENNON AND MCCARTNEY
00843022 .... $16.95

30. BLUES' BEST
00843023 .... $15.99

31. JAZZ IN THREE
00843024 .... $15.99

32. BEST OF SWING
00843025 .... $15.99

33. SONNY ROLLINS
00843029 .... $15.95

34. ALL TIME STANDARDS
00843030 .... $15.99

35. BLUESY JAZZ
00843031 .... $16.99

36. HORACE SILVER
00843032 .... $16.99

37. BILL EVANS
00843033 .... $16.95

38. YULETIDE JAZZ
00843034 .... $16.95

39. "ALL THE THINGS YOU ARE" & MORE JEROME KERN SONGS
00843035 .... $15.99

40. BOSSA NOVA
00843036 .... $15.99

41. CLASSIC DUKE ELLINGTON
00843037 .... $16.99

42. GERRY MULLIGAN FAVORITES
00843038 .... $16.99

43. GERRY MULLIGAN CLASSICS
00843039 .... $16.95

44. OLIVER NELSON
00843040 .... $16.95

45. JAZZ AT THE MOVIES
00843041 .... $15.99

46. BROADWAY JAZZ STANDARDS
00843042 .... $15.99

47. CLASSIC JAZZ BALLADS
00843043 .... $15.99

48. BEBOP CLASSICS
00843044 .... $16.99

49. MILES DAVIS STANDARDS
00843045 .... $16.95

50. GREAT JAZZ CLASSICS
00843046 .... $15.99

51. UP-TEMPO JAZZ
00843047 .... $15.99

52. STEVIE WONDER
00843048 .... $16.99

53. RHYTHM CHANGES
00843049 .... $15.99

54. "MOONLIGHT IN VERMONT" AND OTHER GREAT STANDARDS
00843050 .... $15.99

55. BENNY GOLSON
00843052 .... $15.95

56. "GEORGIA ON MY MIND" & OTHER SONGS BY HOAGY CARMICHAEL
00843056 .... $15.99

57. VINCE GUARALDI
00843057 .... $16.99

58. MORE LENNON AND MCCARTNEY
00843059 .... $15.99

59. SOUL JAZZ
00843060 .... $15.99

60. DEXTER GORDON
00843061 .... $15.95

61. MONGO SANTAMARIA
00843062 .... $15.95

62. JAZZ-ROCK FUSION
00843063 .... $16.99

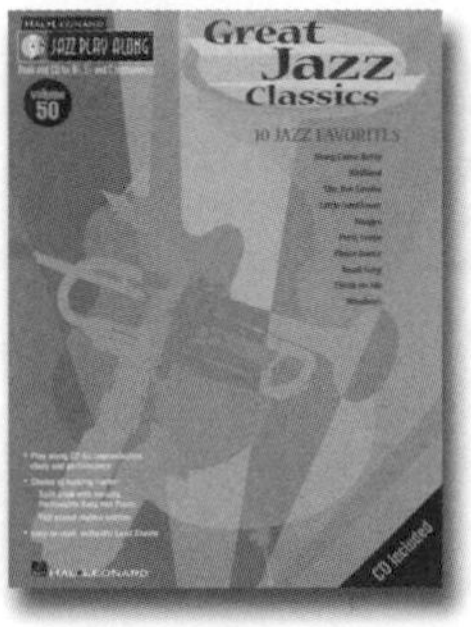

63. CLASSICAL JAZZ
00843064 .... $14.95

64. TV TUNES
00843065 .... $14.95

65. SMOOTH JAZZ
00843066 .... $16.99

66. A CHARLIE BROWN CHRISTMAS
00843067 .... $16.99

67. CHICK COREA
00843068 .... $15.95

68. CHARLES MINGUS
00843069 .... $16.95

69. CLASSIC JAZZ
00843071 .... $15.99

70. THE DOORS
00843072 .... $14.95

71. COLE PORTER CLASSICS
00843073 .... $14.95

72. CLASSIC JAZZ BALLADS
00843074 .... $15.99

73. JAZZ/BLUES
00843075 .... $14.95

74. BEST JAZZ CLASSICS
00843076 .... $15.99

75. PAUL DESMOND
00843077 .... $14.95

76. BROADWAY JAZZ BALLADS
00843078 .... $15.99

77. JAZZ ON BROADWAY
00843079 .... $15.99

78. STEELY DAN
00843070 .... $14.99

79. MILES DAVIS CLASSICS
00843081 .... $15.99

80. JIMI HENDRIX
00843083 .... $15.99

81. FRANK SINATRA – CLASSICS
00843084 .... $15.99

82. FRANK SINATRA – STANDARDS
00843085 .... $15.99

83. ANDREW LLOYD WEBBER
00843104 .... $14.95

84. BOSSA NOVA CLASSICS
00843105 .... $14.95

85. MOTOWN HITS
00843109 .... $14.95

86. BENNY GOODMAN
00843110 .... $14.95

87. DIXIELAND
00843111 .... $14.95

88. DUKE ELLINGTON FAVORITES
00843112 .... $14.95

89. IRVING BERLIN FAVORITES
00843113 .... $14.95

90. THELONIOUS MONK CLASSICS
00841262 .... $16.99

91. THELONIOUS MONK FAVORITES
00841263 .... $16.99

92. LEONARD BERNSTEIN
00450134 .... $15.99

93. DISNEY FAVORITES
00843142 .... $14.99

94. RAY
00843143 .... $14.99

95. JAZZ AT THE LOUNGE
00843144 .... V$14.99

96. LATIN JAZZ STANDARDS
00843145 .... $14.99

97. MAYBE I'M AMAZED*
00843148 .... $15.99

98. DAVE FRISHBERG
00843149 .... $15.99

99. SWINGING STANDARDS
00843150 .... $14.99

100. LOUIS ARMSTRONG
00740423 .... $15.99

101. BUD POWELL
00843152 .... $14.99

102. JAZZ POP
00843153 .... $14.99

103. ON GREEN DOLPHIN STREET & OTHER JAZZ CLASSICS
00843154 .... $14.99

104. ELTON JOHN
00843155 .... $14.99

105. SOULFUL JAZZ
00843151 .... $15.99

106. SLO' JAZZ
00843117 .... $14.99

107. MOTOWN CLASSICS
00843116 .... $14.99

108. JAZZ WALTZ
00843159 .... $15.99

109. OSCAR PETERSON
00843160 .... $16.99

110. JUST STANDARDS
00843161 .... $15.99

111. COOL CHRISTMAS
00843162 .... $15.99

112. PAQUITO D'RIVERA – LATIN JAZZ*
48020662 .... $16.99

113. PAQUITO D'RIVERA – BRAZILIAN JAZZ*
48020663 .... $19.99

114. MODERN JAZZ QUARTET FAVORITES
00843163 .... $15.99

115. THE SOUND OF MUSIC
00843164 .... $15.99

116. JACO PASTORIUS
00843165 .... $15.99

117. ANTONIO CARLOS JOBIM – MORE HITS
00843166 .... $15.99

118. BIG JAZZ STANDARDS COLLECTION
00843167 .... $27.50

119. JELLY ROLL MORTON
00843168 .... $15.99

120. J.S. BACH
00843169 .... $15.99

121. DJANGO REINHARDT
00843170 .... $15.99

122. PAUL SIMON
00843182 .... $16.99

123. BACHARACH & DAVID
00843185 .... $15.99

124. JAZZ-ROCK HORN HITS
00843186 .... $15.99

126. COUNT BASIE CLASSICS
00843157 .... $15.99

127. CHUCK MANGIONE
00843188 .... $15.99

132. STAN GETZ ESSENTIALS
00843193 .... $15.99

133. STAN GETZ FAVORITES
00843194 .... $15.99

134. NURSERY RHYMES*
00843196 .... $17.99

135. JEFF BECK
00843197 .... $15.99

136. NAT ADDERLEY
00843198 .... $15.99

137. WES MONTGOMERY
00843199 .... $15.99

138. FREDDIE HUBBARD
00843200 .... $15.99

139. JULIAN "CANNONBALL" ADDERLEY
00843201 .... $15.99

141. BILL EVANS STANDARDS
00843156 .... $15.99

150. JAZZ IMPROV BASICS
00843195 .... $19.99

151. MODERN JAZZ QUARTET CLASSICS
00843209 .... $15.99

157. HYMNS
00843217 .... $15.99

162. BIG CHRISTMAS COLLECTION
00843221 .... $24.99

Prices, contents, and availability subject to change without notice.

FOR MORE INFORMATION,
SEE YOUR LOCAL MUSIC DEALER,
OR WRITE TO:

HAL•LEONARD®
CORPORATION
7777 W. BLUEMOUND RD. P.O. BOX 13819
MILWAUKEE, WISCONSIN 53213

For complete songlists and more,
visit Hal Leonard online at
www.halleonard.com

*These CDs do not include split tracks.

0811

HAL•LEONARD

BLUES PLAY-ALONG

For use with all the C, B♭, Bass Clef and E♭ Instruments, the Hal Leonard Blues Play-Along Series is the ultimate jamming tool for all blues musicians.

With easy-to-read lead sheets, and other split-track choices on the included CD, these first-of-a-kind packages will bring your local blues jam right into your house! Each song on the CD includes two tracks: a full stereo mix, and a split track mix with removable guitar, bass, piano, and harp parts. The CD is playable on any CD player, and is also enhanced so Mac and PC users can adjust the recording to any tempo without changing the pitch!

1. Chicago Blues
All Your Love (I Miss Loving) • Easy Baby • I Ain't Got You • I'm Your Hoochie Coochie Man • Killing Floor • Mary Had a Little Lamb • Messin' with the Kid • Sweet Home Chicago.
00843106 Book/CD Pack $12.99

2. Texas Blues
Hide Away • If You Love Me Like You Say • Mojo Hand • Okie Dokie Stomp • Pride and Joy • Reconsider Baby • T-Bone Shuffle • The Things That I Used to Do.
00843107 Book/CD Pack $12.99

3. Slow Blues
Don't Throw Your Love on Me So Strong • Five Long Years • I Can't Quit You Baby • I Just Want to Make Love to You • The Sky Is Crying • (They Call It) Stormy Monday (Stormy Monday Blues) • Sweet Little Angel • Texas Flood.
00843108 Book/CD Pack $12.99

4. Shuffle Blues
Beautician Blues • Bright Lights, Big City • Further on up the Road • I'm Tore Down • Juke • Let Me Love You Baby • Look at Little Sister • Rock Me Baby.
00843171 Book/CD Pack $12.99

5. B.B. King
Everyday I Have the Blues • It's My Own Fault Darlin' • Just Like a Woman • Please Accept My Love • Sweet Sixteen • The Thrill Is Gone • Why I Sing the Blues • You Upset Me Baby.
00843172 Book/CD Pack $14.99

6. Jazz Blues
Birk's Works • Blues in the Closet • Cousin Mary • Freddie Freeloader • Now's the Time • Tenor Madness • Things Ain't What They Used to Be • Turnaround.
00843175 Book/CD Pack $12.99

7. Howlin' Wolf
Built for Comfort • Forty-Four • How Many More Years • Killing Floor • Moanin' at Midnight • Shake for Me • Sitting on Top of the World • Smokestack Lightning.
00843176 Book/CD Pack $12.99

8. Blues Classics
Baby, Please Don't Go • Boom Boom • Born Under a Bad Sign • Dust My Broom • How Long, How Long Blues • I Ain't Superstitious • It Hurts Me Too • My Babe.
00843177 Book/CD Pack $12.99

9. Albert Collins
Brick • Collins' Mix • Don't Lose Your Cool • Frost Bite • Frosty • I Ain't Drunk • Master Charge • Trash Talkin'.
00843178 Book/CD Pack $12.99

10. Uptempo Blues
Cross Road Blues (Crossroads) • Give Me Back My Wig • Got My Mo Jo Working • The House Is Rockin' • Paying the Cost to Be the Boss • Rollin' and Tumblin' • Turn on Your Love Light • You Can't Judge a Book by the Cover.
00843179 Book/CD Pack $12.99

11. Christmas Blues
Back Door Santa • Blue Christmas • Dig That Crazy Santa Claus • Merry Christmas, Baby • Please Come Home for Christmas • Santa Baby • Soulful Christmas.
00843203 Book/CD Pack $12.99

12. Jimmy Reed
Ain't That Lovin' You Baby • Baby, What You Want Me to Do • Big Boss Man • Bright Lights, Big City • Going to New York • Honest I Do • You Don't Have to Go • You Got Me Dizzy.
00843204 Book/CD Pack $12.99

FOR MORE INFORMATION, SEE YOUR LOCAL MUSIC DEALER, OR WRITE TO:

HAL•LEONARD® CORPORATION
7777 W. BLUEMOUND RD. P.O. BOX 13819 MILWAUKEE, WI 53213

Prices, content, and availability subject to change without notice.

www.halleonard.com